To Mom
Happy Mother's Day.
Love.
Jiu Lee
1991 —

EARTH
WATER
FIRE
AIR

By Barbara Friedlander Meyer

Illustrated by Jennie Oppenheimer

Designed by John Lynch

PHILOSOPHICAL
LIBRARY
NEW YORK

EARTH
WATER

A

Vegetarian Cookbook

for the 90s

FIRE
AIR

Library of Congress Cataloging-in-Publication Data

Meyer, Barbara Friedlander, 1934–
    Earth, water, fire, air: a vegetarian cookbook for the
nineties
    Barbara Friedlander Meyer: illustrated by Jennie Oppen-
heimer.
        p.   cm.
    ISBN 0-8022-2578-0
    1. Vegetarian cookery.   I. Title.
TX837.M538   1990
641.5'636—dc20   90-6979
                                                        CIP

Copyright © 1990 Barbara Friedlander Meyer
Published by Allied Books Ltd.
31 West 21st Street, New York, N.Y., 10010.
Printed in the United States

This book is dedicated
to the memory of my mother,
Jessie Bankoff Leibowitz,
with great love and gratitude for all
she contributed to me and everyone
else who was fortunate enough
to know her.

Contents

Today, everyone seems to be particularly concerned with eating "light"—less sugar, less dairy products, less fat. In fact, health consciousness, especially in terms of food, is almost commonplace. Nutritional information and breakthroughs have been explosive since the seventies, when I wrote the original version of this book.

In many ways, the book is more relevant now. There are certainly more vegetarians today than in 1972, and they are more knowledgeable and sophisticated. Therefore, many of the ingredients used in the recipes are not as unfamiliar and "exotic" as they probably were then.

Introduction

You will notice that there is no sugar in these recipes; this includes white, brown, raw, turbinado, etc. I have become convinced that certain foods are plain "bad" for you. Sugar is one of the foods to go by the boards in the new healthier eating pattern. Instead, I have substituted honey, pure maple syrup, molasses, brown rice syrup, fruit, fruit juice or fruit concentrates. *All* sweeteners should be used in moderation. Fat should also be consumed in moderation. In addition, the reader is given the option of using oil *or* butter. The additional recipes also reflect other changes in our times. Oriental foods have a prominent place in the new American cuisine—especially vegetarian dishes. Tofu, which was not even mentioned in the original book, can now be purchased in the supermarket. No new vegetarian cookbook would be complete without recipes using this versatile, highly nutritious food. Because there is so much emphasis today on the fiber and weight-reducing potential of grains and other complex carbohydrates, some new recipes for these have been included.

The book is still designed for a broad readership; one need not be a vegetarian to use it. The recipes are also kosher (cheese used must be rennetless and certified as kosher.)

Some statements bear repetition for the new generation of cooks who may be using this book for the first time:

- Forget about the "entrée"; just cook dishes that seem to go well together.
- Be aware of balance in textures, colors, and tastes.
- Remember that protein in a vegetarian meal comes from combining complex carbohydrates, such as grains, with beans, seeds or nuts. These combinations are known as complementary proteins. They need not be in the same dish; just at the same meal. The amounts are not so important, so it doesn't require a scale or a calculator. Just be aware of it and the combinations will come naturally. I have included some more information about complementary proteins on page 12.

Above all, feel free—to experiment; to deviate from a recipe when the spirit moves you; to be creative—and, most important, to enjoy yourself while cooking and eating.

Below are brief descriptions of some of the ingredients called for in the recipes. These items can usually be purchased at natural food stores and most supermarkets. I recommend using them whenever possible, although they are not essential to any recipe.

AGAR-AGAR: Gelatin derived from seaweed, which comes granulated or in the form of bars of pressed flakes. A recipe demonstrating preparation can be found on page 162 (Louise's Kanten).

ARROWROOT: A starch, available in natural food stores in powdered form or in small pieces. Diluted with water or milk, arrowroot is used for thickening soups, sauces, etc. It is a very fine pure vegetable powder and is easier to digest than other starches.

CAROB: Also known as St. John's bread, carob can be used as a substitute for chocolate. It is available in a cocoa-like powder. Use 3 teaspoons of carob powder to 2 tablespoons of water or milk to substitute for 1 square of unsweetened chocolate.

DAIRY PRODUCTS: Natural (unprocessed) and without preservatives. You can make your own yoghurt (see page 183).

DRIED FRUITS: Raw, unfumigated, unsulfured and sun-dried.

EGGS: From organically fed hens; fresh, untreated, fertilized.

GRAIN CEREAL: Cereal with many uses (often interchangeable with flour) made from rolled oats and seeds, nuts, and sometimes fruit. There is a recipe for making it from scratch (see page 180), or it can be purchased under various brand names.

HONEY: Pure, raw, unfiltered.

FLOUR: Stoneground, unfumigated. Those most commonly used are whole-wheat, soy, or corn either alone or in combination.

MARGARINE: May be substituted for butter in any recipe. See OILS for recommended type.

MEAL: Often used interchangeably or combined with flour. Those most commonly used are sunflower, cornmeal, and wheatgerm.

MISO: Paste made by fermenting soybeans, whole-wheat, and sea salt for at least three years. Tamari sauce is a by-product of miso.

MOLASSES: Unsulfured and pure.

NUTS: Raw, without salt or oil. An excellent source of protein. For cooking, toast before use.

OILS (and related products such as margarine, mayonnaise, etc.): Cold pressed, non-hydrogenated, and pure. Some of the greatest nutritional advances have been made regarding the types of recommended oils. Space does not allow for a full discussion of these. Briefly, oils derived from vegetables or seeds should be mechanically (cold) pressed, non-hydrogenated, and contain no artificial colorings, preservatives, or additives. Vegetable oils contain no cholesterol; most contain no fatty acids. "Essential" fatty acids are found in polyunsaturated oil, such as safflower. The American Heart Association recommends that we consume equal amounts of poly- and monosaturated oils (such as olive or canola oil). All oil consumption should be moderate to limit calories.

SALT: Sea salt (made from evaporated sea water), vegetable salt. Note: yeast flavorings such as Marmite may be substituted for salt; also salt-free seasonings.

SEAWEEDS: Dried seaweed is rich in iodine and trace minerals; also high in sodium. Available in natural food and oriental stores, some common seaweeds are wakame, kombu, nori, and dulse. To prepare most seaweeds, soak in water for a few minutes until soft, rinse thoroughly and add to soups, stews, etc. Dulse can be sprinkled on dry as a substitute for salt.

SEEDS: Whole, unfumigated. Sesame seeds in particular are an excellent source of protein.

SPROUTS: Grown from whole and untreated seeds, beans or peas. Sprouts are very rich in vitamins (particularly B-complex) and can be eaten raw or cooked. Those most commonly used are alfalfa, soybean, and mungbean.

TAHINI: Paste made from hulled sesame seeds; also known as sesame butter.

TAMARI SAUCE: Pure soy sauce made from soybeans, water, whole-wheat or wheat-free flour, and sea salt, and aged for at least eighteen months. It is high in protein concentrates and a must in vegetarian diets. Low-sodium tamari is also available.

TEMPEH: Fermented soybean cake, firmer than tofu, with a chicken-like texture. It can be used as a substitute for meat in many dishes. Look for tempeh in the freezer at natural food stores.

TOFU: Curd made from cooked soybeans. Often called "meat without bone," it has been a staple in the Orient for thousands of years. Now it is also popular in the United States, particularly with vegetarians, because of its versatility. Bland by itself, tofu easily picks up desired flavors when combined with other foods or seasonings. It is very rich in B vitamins, high in protein and low in fat, and can be made chewy or soft, grilled, baked, or broiled; creamed for mock cream cheese or blended for mock mayonnaise.

VEGETABLES AND FRUITS: Whenever possible, obtain organically grown and unsprayed produce. For these recipes, all vegetables and fruits should be well-scrubbed and unpeeled, unless otherwise specified. For more information on vegetables, see pages 15–20 and 69.

Here is a brief list of equipment that is particularly useful for many of the recipes in this book:
1. Electric blender (preferably with different speeds for blending, puréeing, chopping, etc.), or food processor.
2. Vegetable steamer. Many types of steamers are available. The simplest is still the collapsible stainless steel steamer basket with legs, which fits into almost any size pan. Bamboo steamers are excellent, as they can be stacked on top of one another over a wok or large pan. They hold a large quantity of vegetables, are easy to clean, and steam efficiently.

COMPLEMENTARY PROTEINS

Protein foods are composed of amino acids. Most amino acids can be made by the body in the presence of sufficient nitrogen. However, there are eight *essential* amino acids which the body cannot produce.

Protein from animal sources (milk, eggs, meat, fish, etc.) contains all the essential amino acids, and is called a "complete protein." Most vegetable protein sources do not contain all eight; by themselves, they are "incomplete proteins." For example: a grain such as brown rice may lack one or two essential amino acids, while a legume (dried bean or peanut) may contain the ones which are missing. By combining them, one obtains a complete protein. Therefore, to be on the safe side, it is advisable for pure vegetarians (eating no animal products,) to combine grains and legumes or grains and nuts.

However, essential amino acids are only necessary for about 20% of *adult* protein needs. (Exceptions are pregnant and nursing women, infants and young children.) It's relatively easy to get the right amount of essential amino acids by just eating more than one or two protein foods. If you eat eggs and dairy products, you need not be concerned. But even if you don't, there are many tasty and simple complementary protein combinations such as:

- brown rice and beans
- corn tortillas and beans
- humus and whole-wheat pita bread
- minestrone soup and whole-wheat bread
- peanut butter and whole-wheat bread sandwich

A Glossary of Vegetables

ARTICHOKES

Preparation: Use whole, hearts and/or bottoms.
Cooking methods: Bake, steam, deep-fry hearts dipped in batter.
Serve hot with sauces, with butter, with lemon, stuffed.
Serve chilled (pre-cooked) marinated, in salads, in sandwiches with dressings, stuffed.

ASPARAGUS

Preparation: Use whole (bottom of stalks removed) or tops only; chop.
Cooking methods: Bake, steam, quick-sauté.*
Serve hot with sauces, with butter, with toasted almonds, baked au gratin.
Serve chilled (pre-cooked) in salads, marinated, with sauces, with dressings, in sandwiches.
Serve raw in salads.

AVOCADOS

Preparation: Cut in half, peel, slice or chop.
Serve raw in salads, in sandwiches, as an appetizer, au vinaigrette, puréed in hot or cold soups and sauces.

BEETS

Preparation: Use whole, with or without stems and tops; slice, chop, grate.
Cooking methods: Steam, boil in soups, bake, deep-fry in batter.
Serve hot with lemon or cream sauce, with butter, in soup (borscht).
Serve chilled (pre-cooked) pickled (with onions), in salads, as an appetizer, in soup (borscht) with sour cream, in preserves.
Serve raw grated in salads (combined with apple or watercress or horseradish).

BROCCOLI

Preparation: Use whole (bottom of stalks removed) or flowerlets.
Cooking methods: Steam, quick-sauté, deep-fry in batter.
Serve hot with melted cheese or Hollandaise sauce, baked au gratin, with yoghurt and wheat germ or chopped nuts, in casseroles, in combination with other vegetables.

Serve chilled (pre-cooked) in salads, in sandwiches, with dressing.
Serve raw as an appetizer, in salads.

BRUSSELS SPROUTS
Preparation: Use whole.
Cooking methods: See BROCCOLI.
Serve hot with chestnuts or water chestnuts; see also BROCCOLI.
Serve chilled (pre-cooked): See BROCCOLI.

CABBAGE
Preparation: Use whole (leaves only); cut in large chunks, shred, chop.
Cooking methods: Steam, quick-sauté, sauté in sauces.
Serve hot with sauces, with apples and/or chestnuts (red cabbage), with noodles, in combination with other vegetables, pickled as sauerkraut, with caraway seeds, stuffed (leaves).
Serve raw juiced, in salads, as cole slaw, pickled as sauerkraut.

16

CARROTS
Preparation: Use whole; slice, grate, curl.
Cooking methods: Steam, quick-sauté, bake by itself or in breads, cakes or cookies, boil in soups, stews or sauces.
Serve hot with butter and/or honey, with sauces, baked au gratin, puréed or whole in soups, with toasted sesame seeds or nuts, in soufflés or custards.
Serve chilled (pre-cooked) in salads, in preserves.
Serve raw juiced, in combination with other vegetables, in salads, in cole slaw, as an appetizer, in ice cream.
Note: Can be grated in tortes and sautéed in breads.

CAULIFLOWER   See BROCCOLI
Note: Also can be stuffed whole and baked.

CELERY
Preparation: Use whole; slice, chop, grate.
Cooking methods: Steam, quick-sauté, braise, boil in soups, stews or sauces.
Serve hot with sauces, in combination with

other vegetables, in casseroles, in soups, in stuffings and fillings, in sauces.
Serve chilled (pre-cooked) with cream sauce.
Serve raw juiced, in salads, in sandwich spreads, plain or stuffed as an appetizer.

CHESTNUTS

Preparation: Use whole or chop.
Cooking methods: Blanch and boil, steam, roast, quick-sauté.
Serve hot in sauces, in combination with other vegetables (particularly cabbage and green beans), puréed in soufflés, in casseroles and stuffings.
Serve chilled (pre-cooked) puréed in puddings and desserts.
Note: Cooked and puréed chestnuts may also be baked in tortes or used as pie fillings.

CHICORY

Preparation: Use whole or torn leaves.
Cooking methods: Steam, braise.
Serve hot with sauces, in combination with other vegetables.
Serve raw in salads (combined with other greens), as a garnish.

CORN

Preparation: Use on cob or kernels alone.
Cooking methods: Steam, boil in soups, stews or sauces, bake.
Serve hot with butter, with sauces, in combination with other vegetables, in casseroles, in puddings, in soups, in fritters.
Note: Raw corn can be ground into meal.

CUCUMBER

Preparation: Slice, chop.
Cooking methods: Steam, boil in soups.
Serve hot with sauce as omelette or pancake filling.
Serve chilled (pre-cooked) puréed in soups.
Serve raw in salads, puréed in soups, in sandwiches and sandwich spreads, pickled, as an appetizer, as a garnish.

DANDELION GREENS

Preparation: Use whole; chop.
Cooking methods: Steam, quick-sauté.
Serve hot with tamari or other sauce.
Serve chilled (pre-cooked) in combination with other vegetables.
Serve raw juiced (combined with celery and carrots), in salads, as a garnish.

EGGPLANT

Preparation: Use whole; cut in half, slice, chop.
Cooking methods: Steam, quick-sauté, boil in stews, deep-fry breaded or in batter, bake.
Serve hot stuffed and baked, baked au gratin or à la parmigiana, in casseroles, combined with other vegetables, puréed in soufflés, with sauces, in stews, mashed.
Serve chilled (pre-cooked) marinated or plain in salads, chopped or mashed as an appetizer.

ENDIVE

Preparation: Use whole (leaves only); slice or chop.
Cooking methods: Steam, braise, bake, quick-sauté.
Serve hot in casseroles, with sauces, in combination with other vegetables, with nuts, in fillings.
Serve raw in salads, in sandwich spreads, in aspics, stuffed.

ESCAROLE See CHICORY
Note: Also can be cooked in soups.

FENNEL See CELERY

GREEN BEANS

Preparation: Use whole; snap, slice, chop.
Cooking methods: Steam, boil in soups and stews, quick-sauté.
Serve hot with butter, sauces, sautéed with sunflower seeds, deep-fried in batter, whole or puréed in soups, in casseroles, in combination with other vegetables.
Serve chilled (pre-cooked) in salads.
Serve raw in salads.

JERUSALEM ARTICHOKES
Preparation: Use whole or slice.
Cooking methods: Steam, bake, quick-sauté, fry.
Serve hot with butter, with sauces, baked au gratin, in soufflés, in soups, mashed.
Serve chilled (pre-cooked) in salads.
Serve raw in salads.

KALE   See SWISS CHARD

KOHLRABI
Preparation: Use whole, with or without leaves; slice, chop, grate.
Cooking methods: Steam, quick-sauté, bake, boil in soups.
Serve hot with butter, with sauces, in soups, stuffed and baked.
Serve chilled (pre-cooked) in salads.
Serve raw in salads.

LEEKS
Preparation: Use white and green parts or white only; chop or slice.
Cooking methods: Steam, boil in soups, braise, quick-sauté.
Serve hot with butter, with sauces, in casseroles, baked au gratin, in soups (usually with potatoes), in custard as pie filling.
Serve chilled (pre-cooked) marinated or plain in salads (combines well with black olives), puréed in soups (vichyssoise).

LETTUCE
Preparation: Use whole or torn leaves; chop.
Cooking methods: Steam, quick-sauté.
Serve hot with sauces, baked au gratin, stuffed and baked, in combination with other vegetables, in fillings.
Serve raw with appetizers, in salads and sandwiches.

LIMA BEANS (GREEN)
Preparation: Shell.
Cooking methods: Steam, bake, boil in soups and stews.
Serve hot with butter, with sauces, baked au

gratin, in casseroles, stews and soups, in combination with other vegetables.

MUSHROOMS
Preparation: Use whole or caps only; slice or chop.
Cooking methods: Quick-sauté, sauté, steam, boil in soups, sauces and stews, grill, broil, bake, deep-fry in batter.
Serve hot in or with sauces, with butter, in casseroles, soups and stews, in combination with rice, pasta or other vegetables (particularly onions), in soufflés, stuffed or in fillings or stuffings.
Serve chilled (pre-cooked) in appetizers, salads and sandwiches, puréed in pâté, as an appetizer.
Serve raw plain or marinated in salads and appetizers.

OKRA
Preparation: Use whole (stems removed) or chop.
Cooking methods: Steam, boil in stews and soups, quick-sauté.
Serve hot with sauces, in soups and stews, in casseroles, in combination with other vegetables (particularly tomatoes).
Note: Okra powder is used as a thickener for soups and sauces. Okra slices may be strung and dried for use as a spice in stews and soups.

ONIONS
Preparation: Use whole; slice, chop, grate.
Cooking methods: Quick-sauté, sauté, steam, boil in soups, stews and sauces, braise, bake, broil, fry, deep-fry in batter.
Serve hot with butter, in or with sauces, in casseroles, in stews, and soups, stuffed, in fillings or stuffings, in pancakes, in combination with other vegetables.
Serve chilled (pre-cooked) in appetizers and sandwiches, puréed in pâté.
Serve raw plain or marinated in salads and appetizers, in sandwiches, as a garnish.
Note: Onion powder or onion salt is used as a seasoning.

PARSNIPS
Preparation: Remove leaves; slice, chop, grate.
Cooking methods: Steam, quick-sauté, deep-fry, boil in soups and stews.
Serve hot with butter, with sauces, mashed with other vegetables (particularly potatoes).
Serve chilled (pre-cooked) in salads.
Serve raw grated in mayonnaise, in salads.

PEAS (GREEN)
Preparation: Shell.
Cooking methods: Steam, quick-sauté, boil in soups, stews, and sauces, bake.
Serve hot with butter, with sauces, in pastry shells, in casseroles, puréed in soufflés, whole or puréed in soups, in combination with other vegetables (particularly onions).
Serve chilled (pre-cooked) in salads and appetizers.
Serve raw in salads.

PEPPERS (SWEET GREEN)
Preparation: Use whole; cut in quarters, slice, chop.
Cooking methods: Steam, quick-sauté, sauté, fry, deep-fry in batter, boil in stews and sauces, bake, broil.
Serve hot with sauces, stuffed and baked, in casseroles, in stews and sauces, fried, in stuffings or fillings, in combination with other vegetables, pasta or rice.
Serve chilled (pre-cooked) in salads, appetizers, and sandwich spreads.
Serve raw in salads, sandwiches, and appetizers, as an appetizer (stuffed).

PIMIENTOS   See PEPPERS

POTATOES (WHITE AND SWEET)
Preparation: Use whole; cut in quarters, slice, chop, grate.
Cooking methods: Steam, boil, sauté, fry, deep-fry alone, in batter or in pancakes, bake, roast.
Serve hot with butter, with sauces, mashed, in combination with other vegetables, baked (plain or stuffed), as dumplings or pancakes, in puddings, in casseroles, soups, stuffings and stews, mashed and fried.

Serve chilled (pre-cooked) as a salad.
Note: Cooked and puréed potatoes may be baked with flour into rolls and bread.

PUMPKINS See SQUASH
Note: Also can be mashed and baked in pie.

RADISHES
Preparation: Use whole; slice, chop, grate.
Serve raw juiced (combined with celery), in salads, as appetizers (black radishes, grated), in sandwiches.

SORREL See WATERCRESS

SPINACH
Preparation: Use whole leaves and stems or leaves only; tear or chop.
Cooking methods: Steam, quick-sauté, deep-fry in batter, boil in soups.
Serve hot with butter, with sauces, puréed in soufflés and puddings, baked au gratin, in pies and casseroles, in combination with other vegetables, pasta or rice, in fillings, soups, and dumplings.
Serve raw juiced (combined with carrots and celery), in salads, plain or marinated, in mayonnaise.

SQUASH (YELLOW, BUTTERNUT, WINTER, ACORN)
Preparation: Use whole; slice, chop, grate.
Cooking methods: Steam, quick-sauté, bake, boil in soups and stews, broil.
Serve hot with butter, with sauces, in stews, and casseroles, sliced or puréed in soups, stuffed and baked, in combination with other vegetables, dried beans, rice or pasta, mashed.
Serve chilled (pre-cooked) in salads, as an appetizer, puréed in custards.
Serve raw in salads and appetizers, mixed with cream cheese in sandwich spreads.

SWISS CHARD
Preparation: Use leaves and stems; chop.
Cooking methods: Quick-sauté, steam, boil in soups.

Serve hot with butter, with sauces, in soups, in combination with other vegetables.

TOMATOES
Preparation: Use whole; slice or chop.
Cooking methods: Steam, quick-sauté, grill, broil, bake, boil in soups, stews and sauces.
Serve hot with sauces, stuffed and baked, in stuffings and fillings, in casseroles, soups, stews and sauces, puréed in soufflés, in combination with other vegetables, pasta or rice.
Serve chilled (pre-cooked) in appetizers, marinated, stuffed.
Serve raw juiced, in salads, marinated, stuffed, in sandwiches and appetizers.

TURNIPS
Preparation: Use whole, with or without leaves; slice or grate.
Cooking methods: Steam, quick-sauté, bake, fry, boil in soups and stews.
Serve hot with butter, with sauces, in soups and stews, stuffed and baked, deep-fried in batter, mashed, in combination with other vegetables (particularly potatoes).

WATERCRESS
Preparation: Use whole leaves and stems or leaves only; chop.
Cooking methods: Steam, quick-sauté, boil in soups, bake.
Serve hot with sauces, in combination with other vegetables, puréed in hot or cold soups.
Serve raw juiced (combined with carrots and celery), in salads, in appetizers, in sandwiches and sandwich spreads, as a garnish.

ZUCCHINI
Preparation: Use whole; slice, chop, grate.
Cooking methods: Steam, quick-sauté, deep-fry breaded or in batter, broil, bake.
Serve hot with sauces, stuffed and baked, in casseroles, in combination with other vegetables, in fillings, baked or broiled au gratin.
Serve chilled (pre-cooked) as an appetizer, in salads and appetizers.
Serve raw in salads.

Herbs can perform magic with so many foods. They add special substance to vegetarian cooking. Experimentation is the key word—the flavors you can create are virtually limitless, and the guide below should be used merely as a starting point. Herbs can be blended together and added to food in two ways: mixed directly in; or tied together (in a cloth bag if dried herbs are being used), immersed during cooking and removed before serving.

Most herbs can be purchased in stores if you do not have the space nor the inclination to grow them. You may be able to buy some fresh, in season, but often they will be dried and packed. Buy in small quantities—once

A Glossary of Herbs

dried, they tend to lose flavor quickly. As dried herbs are more concentrated, use ½ to ¼ of the quantity for fresh herbs. *One word of advice:* No more than two courses of any one meal should be flavored with herbs.

Growing herbs from seed is very simple and enjoyable. A few feet of garden or a shelf (in a sunny place) to hold eight or ten small pots is all you need. Indoors, these herbs can be planted at any time: dill, chives, basil, parsley, marjoram, thyme, sage, oregano, mint. When grown, the herbs may be cut and used as needed, or dried and stored. Cutting often encourages growth, and your indoor herb garden may serve you year-round. Some companies now distribute indoor herb gardens complete with pots, seeds and directions.

For an outdoor garden, either plant seeds or transplant seedlings (sown indoors) in the spring.

A list of the most commonly used herbs follows. Planting instructions are given for those that are easy to cultivate.

BASIL
Use in: Cheese spreads, soups, tomato dishes, eggs, cheese soufflés, beans, eggplant, onions, peas, squash, stuffings, salads, aspics.
Planting instructions: This is an annual and should be planted in early spring in a sunny place. Cut frequently when full grown.

BAY LEAVES
Use in: Soups, eggs, sauces, beets, carrots, potatoes, stewed tomatoes, custards.

CHERVIL
Use in: Avocado and cheese spreads, soups, garnish for soups, all vegetable salads, butter and cream sauces, eggs, beets, eggplant, peas, potatoes, spinach, tomatoes; add to melted butter for vegetables.

CHIVES
Use interchangeably with onions; chives are milder.
Planting instructions: Grow in window-box. Cut often.

DILL WEED
Use in: Pickling, cheese dips and spreads, stuffed eggs, salad dressing, salads, soups, beets, spinach, broccoli, Brussels sprouts, sauerkraut, beans, turnips, potatoes.
Planting instructions: This is an annual and should be planted in the spring in a sunny place.

GARLIC
Use in: Everything as desired. Also obtainable dehydrated as a powder and in salt.

MARJORAM

Use in: Cheese dips and spreads, eggs, soups, mixed green salads, fruit salads, sauces, stuffings, Brussels sprouts, squash, peas, spinach, carrots, zucchini, kale, fruit juices.

Planting instructions: This is a perennial and should be planted in the spring in southern climates; elsewhere, it should be sown indoors and transplanted in the spring. Cut off and dry entire flower when it appears.

OREGANO

Use in: Mushrooms, avocado dips, cheese spreads, juices, salads, soups, sauces (particularly in Italian-style dishes), eggs, broccoli, lentils, mushrooms, onions, tomatoes, cabbage.

Planting instructions: Plant in the spring in a sunny place.

PARSLEY

Use in: Cheese and avocado dips and spreads, garnish for soups, sauces, eggs, salads; cook in vegetable soups, stews; juice (combined with carrots and celery).

Planting instructions: This is a biennial and should be planted in the spring.

PEPPERMINT

Use in: Beverages, juices, tea, garnish for fruit salads and desserts, bean and pea soups, sauces, fruit and yoghurt dressing, vegetable, Waldorf and cole slaw salads, cream cheese, carrots, peas, potatoes, spinach, zucchini.

Planting instructions: Plant in rich, moist soil in the spring. It is a perennial and grows like a weed; it should be controlled.

ROSEMARY

Use in: Fruit salads, jam, beverages, soups (particularly in pea, potato, and spinach soups), sauces, eggs, cauliflower, cucumber, mushrooms, peas, potatoes, spinach, and green salads.

Planting instructions: A perennial; transplant seedlings in spring to a dry sunny place.

SAFFRON

Use in: Butter, eggs, cream cheese, squash, zucchini, rice (paella), frostings, fruit juices, sweet buns, cakes.

SAGE

Use in: Sharp cheese spreads, butter and cheese sauces, cottage cheese, creamed eggs and soufflés, carrots, eggplant, lima beans, onions, peas, tomatoes, soups.

Planting instructions: This is a perennial and should be planted in the spring in sandy or dry soil.

SUMMER SAVORY

Use in: Cheese spreads, eggs, tomato and vegetable juices, soups, salads, sauces, horseradish, artichokes, asparagus, beans, lentils, rice, sauerkraut, stewed pears.

Planting instructions: This is an annual and should be planted in the spring in a sunny place. Thin to 6 inches apart. When the flowers appear, cut and dry the entire plant.

TARRAGON

Use in: Cheese spreads, cottage cheese, juices, soups, green salads, eggs, cole slaw, fruit, sauces and salad dressings, celery, mushrooms, potatoes, spinach, tomatoes.

Planting instructions: This is a perennial. Plant only from cuttings in the spring in a fairly shady spot. Protect plants in the fall.

THYME

Use in: Borscht (beet soup), soups, aspics, beet and tomato salads, cole slaw, sauces, cottage cheese, eggs, asparagus, beans, beets, carrots, onions, zucchini, mushrooms, custards, fruit compotes, vegetable and tomato juices.

Planting instructions: This is a perennial and should be planted in a dry sunny spot in the spring.

C H A P T E R

1

Raw vegetables and fruits should be part of everyone's daily diet. Salads provide a delicious health boost and, when served at the beginning of the meal, stimulate the appetite and aid the digestion.

Salad vegetables and fruits should be as fresh and crisp as possible. Dry greens well and store in the refrigerator in tightly closed containers or plastic bags until ready to use. Then wash and dry thoroughly. Prepare salad ingredients at the last minute to retain their vitamins.

Unless otherwise specified, dressings should

Salads

be added just before serving. Do not drown salads. A good rule is to use *less* dressing than is required if you are in doubt.

Wooden salad bowls should not be washed—just wipe them clean.

You will be surprised at how creative salad-making can be. For instance, try adding cooked, leftover vegetables such as parsnips; or something unique like raw asparagus or dandelion leaves. I hope the following recipes will whet your appetite for putting together a great variety of possible salads.

ARTICHOKE AND EGG IN MAYONNAISE

serving: 2
preparation time: 5 minutes

1 large artichoke, cooked and chilled
2 tablespoons mayonnaise
2 hard-cooked eggs, chilled
2 tablespoons chopped fresh dill or
      parsley
2 slices pimiento

1. Divide artichoke in half and fill each
   half with 1 tablespoon mayonnaise.
2. Slice eggs and cover each artichoke
   half with egg slices. Top with herb
   and pimiento slice. Serve chilled on a
   bed of lettuce.

28

CUCUMBER AND YOGHURT SALAD

servings: 4
preparation time: 1½ hours

  2 large cucumbers, sliced very thin
  2 cups yoghurt
1½ teaspoons turmeric
  2 tablespoons chopped fresh mint or
     1 tablespoon dried mint

1. Place cucumber slices in a deep bowl.
2. Separately, blend yoghurt, turmeric, and mint together.
3. Pour over cucumber and toss very well.
4. Chill for at least one hour. Dressing should be pale green. Serve very cold.

NOTE
This salad is a delicious accompaniment to bean dishes and curried dishes.

VARIATION
With the addition of vegetable broth, this becomes a refreshing summer soup.

GRAPEFRUIT AND AVOCADO SALAD

servings: 4
preparation time: 10 minutes

> 2 grapefruits, peeled, sectioned, and
>   cut
> 2 avocados, peeled and sliced

DRESSING:
> ½ cup olive oil
>   juice of 1 lemon
>   salt and pepper to taste
> 1 tablespoon light sweet cream
>   (optional)

1. Mix grapefruit sections and avocado slices together.
2. Blend dressing. Toss well and serve chilled.

VARIATION
In place of lemon-oil dressing, substitute chilled Miso and Tahini Sauce (see page 149).

MIXED-FRUIT SALAD

servings: 4
preparation time: 25 minutes

    1 melon,* cubed or scooped small
    1 cup strawberries, stems removed
        and cut in half
    2 oranges, peeled and sliced
        horizontally
    2 apples or pears, sliced
    1 banana, sliced

DRESSING
    2 tablespoons tahini (sesame butter)
    2 tablespoons honey
    4 tablespoons yoghurt
    ¼ cup chopped toasted almonds
    ¼ cup currants
       juice of ½ lemon (optional)

    1. Combine all fruits in a bowl.
    2. Blend dressing well and toss with
       fruits. Allow to stand at least 15
       minutes before serving.

*Any melon in season (except water-
melon) may be used.

VARIATION
Other fruits in season can be combined
beautifully. For instance, substitute
another berry (such as blueberries) for
strawberries; peaches for melon. The only
"rule" is that there should be at least
one citrus fruit and one hard fruit (apple
or pear). The rest is up to you!

MEDITERRANEAN SALAD

servings: 4
preparation time: 10 minutes

    1 large head romaine lettuce (see
      NOTE on page 36)
    2 scallions or green onions, chopped
      fine
    1 orange, thinly sliced horizontally
    ½ cup black olives, pitted and sliced
    ½ cup hard cheese, cubed
    1 tablespoon each sage and basil
    4 hard-cooked eggs, chilled and sliced
      in half lengthwise

1. Combine all ingredients, adding eggs
   last.
2. Toss well with Mayonnaise Dressing
   (see page 156). Serve chilled.

TOMATO, SCALLIONS, AND AVOCADO SALAD

servings: 4
preparation time: 1½ hours

  6 tomatoes
  4 scallions, diced
    pinch of salt
  1 avocado, sliced

DRESSING
  1 teaspoon lemon juice
  1 tablespoon olive oil
  ½ teaspoon salt
    pinch each of dry mustard and
      pepper
  1 teaspoon chopped chervil

1. Dip tomatoes in boiling water, re-move quickly, and peel off skins. Slice thickly.
2. Place scallions in bottom of a dish. Add tomato slices and salt. Allow to stand in a cool place for at least one hour.
3. When ready to serve, blend dressing ingredients; add avocado and toss well with dressing. Serve chilled.

STUFFED TOMATOES

servings: 4
preparation time: 1½ hours

  4 large tomatoes
    salt to taste
  2 bunches parsley, pounded fine
  2 tablespoons olive oil
  4 garlic cloves, pressed

1. Cut tops off tomatoes, scoop out centers, and salt the insides. Turn upside down to drain thoroughly.
2. Combine parsley, olive oil, and garlic.
3. Divide parsley mixture into four equal parts and fill tomatoes. Allow to stand in a cool place for one hour or longer. Serve chilled on lettuce leaves.

EXOTIC GREEN WALNUT SALAD

servings: 6–8
preparation time: at least 1½ hours

    1 pound green walnuts*
    1 bottle white grape juice
    1 shallot, diced fine
    pepper to taste

1. Remove skins and cut walnuts in half.
2. Place in a bowl and cover with grape juice, shallot, and pepper.
3. Allow to stand in a cool place and marinate for one hour or longer.
4. Serve cool on bed of lettuce and orange slices.

*Available in specialty and gourmet food shops.

MANY-VEGETABLES SALAD

servings: 4
preparation time: 10 minutes

1 large head romaine lettuce
1 cauliflower, broken into flowerlets
2 scallions, sliced
6 cooked artichoke hearts, sliced in
   half
6 radishes, sliced thin
1 cup cooked chick peas
   handful of alfalfa sprouts
   handful of toasted sesame seeds
2 pimientos, sliced thin
2 tomatoes, sliced thin

1. Tear—do not cut—lettuce into small pieces.
2. Combine with all other ingredients, adding tomatoes last.
3. Toss well with French Dressing (see page 157). Dressing should lightly cover—not drown—salad. Serve immediately.

NOTE
Lettuce is best when dry and crisp. If too wet, put individual leaves in a tightly closed plastic bag and place in the freezer for a few minutes just before preparation.

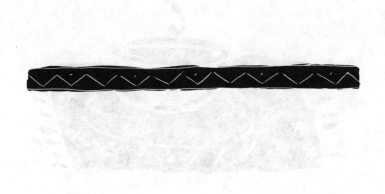

CHAPTER

2

Soups are so versatile! A good soup can get a meal off to a great start—or it can be a meal in itself. When cooking soup, be generous with herbs; also, use the outer leaves of vegetables like carrots, celery, and cabbage (and discards from salad greens). Soups benefit greatly from the use of leftover vegetables, appropriate sauces, etc.

The stock for vegetable soup may be water in which vegetables have been previously steamed; or in which beans or grains have been soaked. The term "vegetable broth" refers to homemade stock or any instant vegetable concentrate—powder, packets, or cubes (but no MSG,

Soups

please!)—diluted in water. Vegetable broth may be substituted for water in all soup recipes (except fruit soup).

Any soup can be thickened in the following manner: Heat a small pan, mix 2 tablespoons oil (or butter) with 2 tablespoons flour (or cornstarch or arrowroot) and stir until brown; then add a small amount of soup liquid and stir until smooth. Add to soup and heat through before serving. For cream soups, milk or cream may be added to the flour mixture.

Soup may be garnished with such diverse items as parsley, watercress, chives; or buttered croutons; or toasted chick peas.

FRESH ASPARAGUS SOUP

servings: 4–6
preparation time: 40 minutes

        6 cups water
    1½ pounds asparagus, sliced diagonally 1
            inch long
        2 egg yolks, beaten
        1 tablespoon cornstarch or arrowroot
            salt and pepper to taste
            pinch of rosemary
        2 tablespoons heavy sweet or sour
            cream (optional)

1. In a large pot, bring salted water to a boil, add asparagus, and cook over low heat until tender, yet still crisp. Remove from water and place on a plate.
2. Combine egg yolks and cornstarch or arrowroot and pour slowly into water. Stir continuously, over low heat, until liquid is smooth and creamy. Add seasoning and asparagus. Simmer until asparagus is well cooked.
3. If desired, stir in two tablespoons heavy sweet or sour cream just before serving. Serve hot.

COLD QUICK "REAL" BORSCHT

servings: 4
preparation time: 10 minutes

    1 large jar pickled beets, chilled
    1 large jar plain beets, chilled
    1 large can vegetable juice, chilled
    3 tablespoons chopped fresh dill
       sour cream

1. Pour beets and beet liquid into blender and chop.
2. Pour in juice and blend well.
3. Serve chilled, topped with dill and sour cream.

SWEET CREAM OF CARROT SOUP

servings: 4
preparation time: 50 minutes

1 pound carrots, chopped
4 cups water or vegetable broth
salt and pepper to taste
1 teaspoon honey
1 egg yolk
4 tablespoons light sweet cream
1 tablespoon butter

1. Bring carrots and water or broth to a boil. Cover pot, lower heat, and simmer for approximately ½ hour.
2. When carrots are tender, remove them from water and purée either in a food mill or blender. Return carrots to water and bring to a boil.
3. Add seasoning and honey.
4. Beat egg yolk and cream together in a small bowl.
5. Remove soup from heat and slowly stir in egg mixture and butter. Heat through but do not boil. Serve hot or cold.

NOTE
Any soup can be "creamed" without using dairy products in the following manner: Substitute oil for butter, and instead of using milk or cream, use cashews—the amount will depend on how "creamy" you want the soup. Simply blend the nuts with a little water or broth until smooth, add to soup and cook for about 15 minutes.

COLD FRESH CHERRY SOUP

servings: 4
preparation time: 25 minutes (not including chilling)

1½ pounds sour cherries, stems
     removed
3 eggs, separated
2 tablespoons honey or brown rice
     syrup
4 cups water
1 lemon rind, sliced

1. Boil cherries for 15 minutes.
2. Meanwhile, beat egg yolks with sweetener until pale yellow and creamy. Then pour slowly into soup, stirring constantly.
3. Whip egg whites until stiff and fold in carefully.
4. Add lemon rind. Taste and add more sweetener if necessary.
5. Chill and remove rind before serving.

VARIATION
For a richer soup, just before serving, add 2 tablespoons sour cream and beat well. For a thinner soup, increase amount of water. Plums or peaches may be substituted for cherries.

SPICY INDIAN DAHL SOUP

servings: 8
preparation time: 1 hour

　8 cups water
　1 cup yellow split peas
¼ potato, peeled and grated
　3 potatoes, peeled and sliced thick
　　oil or clarified butter (ghee)
　1 teaspoon mustard seed
¾ teaspoon cumin
¾ teaspoon coriander
　2 teaspoons turmeric
½ teaspoon cayenne
　1 teaspoon salt

1. Boil split peas and grated potato in water until peas are soft. Then purée with a beater and add sliced potatoes. Lower heat.
2. While soup is cooking, cover bottom of small frying pan with oil or ghee and toast mustard seeds until they pop. Mix in other spices and stir well.
3. Pour a small amount of soup liquid into pan very carefully to avoid splattering. Stir well and pour soup-spice mixture back into soup.
4. Simmer until potatoes are cooked. Serve hot.

MENU SUGGESTIONS
Serve with Chapattis (see page 132) and Cucumber and Yoghurt Salad (see page 29).

QUICK COLD GAZPACHO

servings: 4
preparation time: 15 minutes (not including chilling)

1 green pepper, cut in quarters
4 tomatoes, cut in quarters
½ small cucumber, cut in half
1 small onion, cut in half
6 garlic cloves, cut in half
1 cup olive oil
¼ cup vinegar
3 hard rolls or 4 pieces stale bread,
    soaked in water
salt to taste

1. Purée first five ingredients in a
   blender or food mill. Add oil and
   vinegar and continue to blend.
2. Break off small pieces of rolls or
   bread, squeeze out a little water, and
   add to blender. Continue blending
   until all bread is used up. Add salt.
3. Strain. If soup tastes too strong, add
   cold water. Chill and serve with garnishes.

GARNISHES
  1 small onion, diced fine
  ½ small cucumber, diced fine
  1 green pepper, diced fine
    croutons

MISO SOUP

servings: 6–8
preparation time: 1 hour

2 strips well dried sea weed, either wakame or kombu (optional)
2 medium onions, cut in wedges like orange segments
2 tablespoons oil
2 carrots, sliced thin
½ cabbage, shredded
2 quarts stock water or vegetable broth
3 tablespoons miso paste, more or less depending on desired strength
chopped scallions

1. Soak seaweed for several minutes. Rinse well to get rid of any dirt. Snip into small pieces.
2. In a large pot, sauté onions in oil for 5 minutes, until they begin to turn translucent.
3. Add carrots and continue to sauté until carrots are coated or shiny.
4. Add cabbage and continue to sauté. Add a little more oil if necessary, but not so much as to make soup greasy.
5. Add stock and bring to a boil. Then add seaweed and cook 30–45 minutes, until cabbage and carrots are done, but not mushy. Turn off heat.
6. Combine an equal amount of soup stock with the miso and mix well, trying to crush beans in miso if possible. (You can put them through a sieve.)
7. Add miso mixture to soup and leave covered away from the heat for 5 minutes.
8. Stir well and taste. Add more miso if desired. Serve garnished with a few chopped scallions. You may reheat over low heat but *don't* bring to a boil at any time after miso is added. Temperatures of 200 degrees will start to kill the valuable enzymes in miso.

VARIATIONS
You can substitute other root vegetables like daikon (oriental radish) or winter squash for carrots and add other greens like kale or radish tops. Try to combine vegetables that have the same cooking time, e.g. summer squash, radish tops, and dulse (seaweed) in the summer; daikon and kale in winter.

POTATO SOUP

servings: 6
preparation time: 1 hour

4 large potatoes, peeled and cut in
    small chunks
1 large onion or 2 leeks, diced
2 garlic cloves, minced
    salt and pepper to taste
6 cups water
2 tablespoons butter
2 tablespoons flour
    pinch of paprika
1 bunch cilantro, chopped (optional)

1. Slowly boil potatoes, onion, carrot,
   salt, and pepper in water for approximately ¾ hour.
2. In a frying pan, melt butter over low
   heat. Add flour and stir continuously
   until darkly browned. Be careful not
   to burn!
3. Remove pan from heat and gradually add one ladleful of soup liquid,
   stirring until smooth; use a beater, if
   necessary.
4. Add flour mixture and paprika to
   soup, stir well, and bring to a boil.
   Serve hot.

MENU SUGGESTION
Serve with Artichoke and Egg in Mayonnaise (see page 28).

VARIATION
This soup can be put in the blender for a
creamier consistency. It may also be
served cold.

MUSHROOM, BEAN, AND BARLEY SOUP

servings: 6
preparation time: 2 hours

1 large onion, diced
1 garlic clove, minced
2 tablespoons butter or oil
½ pound mushrooms, sliced
6 cups vegetable broth, boiling
½ cup dried lima beans, soaked for
    several hours
1 cup barley
1 bunch parsley, chopped fine
    pinch each of nutmeg, thyme, and
      ginger
1 clove
    salt and pepper to taste

1. In a large pot, sauté onion and garlic in butter or oil until golden.
2. Add mushrooms, lower heat, and cook covered for 10 minutes.
3. Add broth and remaining ingredients. Cover and simmer for 1½ hours. Serve hot.

NOTE
A dark broth adds richness to this soup. If a thinner soup is desired, add more broth.

VARIATION
To turn this into a cream soup, make Basic Cream Sauce (see page 146) using 1 tablespoon butter, 1 tablespoon flour, and 1 cup milk. Mix with a little broth, stir into soup, and heat through just before serving.

MENU SUGGESTION
Serve with French Green Beans and Sunflower Seeds (see page 77).

ALL-GREEN-VEGETABLE SOUP

servings: 4
preparation time: 45 minutes

    2 tablespoons oil or butter
    1 onion, sliced
    1 garlic clove, minced
    2 celery stalks and leaves, chopped
    4 cups vegetable broth
  ½ pound each string beans and peas
    1 bunch parsley, chopped fine
    1 bay leaf
    2 sprigs each rosemary and thyme
      pinch of nutmeg
      salt and pepper to taste

1. Sauté onion and garlic in oil or butter until golden. Add celery and stir for a few minutes. Drain off any excess oil.
2. Meanwhile, snap beans in half and shell peas.
3. In a large pot, bring broth to a boil and add all ingredients. Bring to a boil again; cover and simmer until beans and peas are tender.
4. Remove bay leaf and stalks of herbs. Adjust seasoning and serve hot.

VEGETABLE SOUP WITH WHEAT BERRY

servings: 6–8
preparation time: at least 2 hours

2 tablespoons butter or oil
1 large onion, diced
3 celery stalks, diced
1 small cabbage, shredded
1 cup wheat berry
8 cups vegetable broth, boiling
3 carrots, sliced
1 turnip, sliced
1 cup chopped parsley
1 clove
1 bay leaf
   pinch of nutmeg
   salt and pepper to taste

1. In a large pot, sauté onions, celery, and cabbage in butter or oil until golden. Add wheat berry, stirring constantly, until grain is lightly browned.
2. Add broth to pot, cover, and simmer over low heat for ½ hour.
3. Add remaining vegetables and seasoning. Cover pot again and simmer for 1 hour or longer, until vegetables are thoroughly cooked and wheat berry is soft, but not mushy. This is a thick soup. It can be made thinner by adding more broth and adjusting seasoning accordingly. Remove bay leaf before serving. Serve hot, topped with buttered croutons.

VARIATION
The recipe above can be revised to make a delicious puréed vegetable soup as follows: Use all the same ingredients, but substitute 1 cup green split peas for wheat berry and add peas to broth at the same time as other vegetables. When all vegetables are cooked, remove pot from heat and allow to cool slightly. Then remove bay leaf and spoon all vegetables, together with enough water to blend smoothly, into blender. Purée well and return to pot. Toss in 1 cup of toasted chick peas (optional) and simmer for approximately 15 minutes. Serve hot.

MENU SUGGESTION
Serve with Tomato, Scallions, and Avocado Salad (see page 33).

50

CREAM OF WATERCRESS SOUP

servings: 6
preparation time: 50 minutes

4 tablespoons butter
1 garlic clove, minced
1 onion or 2 leeks, chopped
6 potatoes, peeled and sliced thin
   salt and pepper to taste
1 cup water
1 bunch watercress
2½ cups water
1½ cups milk
2 egg yolks
½ cup light sweet cream

1. In a large pot, sauté garlic and onion or leeks in butter until golden.
2. Add potatoes, seasoning, and one cup of water. Cover and boil; then reduce heat and cook until potatoes are almost tender, approximately 15 minutes.
3. Reserve half the watercress leaves. Add remaining leaves and stems, milk and water. Simmer for 15 minutes; then remove and purée in food mill or blender. Return to pot.
4. Blend egg yolks and cream together. Gradually add to soup, stirring continuously, until soup is slightly thickened. Heat through, but do not boil.
5. Spoon into bowls and top with reserved watercress leaves. Serve hot or chilled.

51

VARIATION
If you want a light or dairy-free soup, replace butter with oil, omit milk and sweet cream. Blend in cashews or tofu.

CHAPTER

3

Eggs and cheese have an important function in a vegetarian diet, for they provide necessary protein. Besides their obvious food value, they are among the most versatile and attractive of ingredients. Cheese can appear gracefully at any point of the meal, as appetizer, salad, main course, or dessert.

Try to use fresh, untreated eggs from organically fed hens. The difference in taste may

Eggs, Cheese, and Pasta

astound you! *Important:* Refrigerate eggs immediately and cook them slowly to retain their flavor.

Try to purchase noodles, macaroni and spaghetti made from stone-ground whole-grain flours. Whole-wheat noodles add a unique texture and flavor to any pasta dish.

Most kinds of pasta may be interchanged in any of the following recipes.

BAKED EGGS A LA FLAMENCO

servings: 4
preparation time: 40 minutes

   2 potatoes, diced small
   2 tablespoons olive oil
   1 cup peas, cooked
   4 pimientos, diced
   ½ pound asparagus, cooked (optional)
   2 cups homemade or canned tomato
       sauce
   8 eggs
     salt to taste

1. Fry potatoes as for Miguel's Authentic Spanish Omelette (see page 58).
2. Preheat oven to 325°.
3. Grease four small casseroles and line with fried potatoes. Add remaining vegetables in separate layers and pour tomato sauce over everything.
4. For each casserole, break two eggs into a bowl and slide carefully on top.
5. Bake for 15–20 minutes, until whites have set. Salt after baking and serve straight from the oven.

MENU SUGGESTION
Serve with Mediterranean Salad (see page 32).

BUTTERLESS SCRAMBLED EGGS

servings: 2
preparation time: 8–10 minutes

    4 tablespoons milk
    3 eggs
    salt and pepper to taste

1. In a frying pan, heat milk to the boiling point; then lower heat.
2. Beat eggs with salt and pepper and add to milk. Stir, cover, and let cook for approximately 3 minutes. Serve on warmed plates.

55

EGGS A LA RUSSE

servings: 4
preparation time: 5 minutes

    4 hard-cooked eggs, chilled and sliced
        in half lengthwise
    1 small jar red caviar
    2 lemons, sliced thin

DRESSING
    6 tablespoons mayonnaise
    2 tablespoons chili sauce or 2
        tablespoons ketchup mixed with 1
        teaspoon relish
    1 teaspoon chopped chives

1. Blend all dressing ingredients well.
2. On a bed of lettuce, place 2 egg
   halves; spoon dressing over them.
   Top with caviar.
3. Serve chilled with lemon slices as an
   appetizer or salad.

PLAIN AND FILLED OMELETTES

servings: 2
preparation time: varies with omelette

4 eggs
2 tablespoons butter
1 tablespoon light sweet cream (optional)
   tional)
   dash of vanilla
   salt and pepper to taste

1. Beat eggs, cream (if used), and seasoning until eggs are pale yellow and foamy.
2. Heat an omelette pan* and melt butter over low heat.
3. Pour eggs in pan, moving pan back and forth with one hand, stirring eggs with a fork in a circular motion with the other hand. Continue until bottom of eggs are set and tops are moist. If a filling is used (see below), place it on one half of the omelette—the side nearest you. Tilt the pan back slightly and roll the omelette with a fork or spatula away from you. When rolled, turn omelette quickly onto a warmed plate.

FILLINGS
Omelettes can be made with a variety of fillings; here are a few samples.
Cheddar or Swiss cheese: Use ½ cup, grated.
Mushrooms: Use 5 or 6, sliced and sautéed in butter, with or without Cream Sauce (see page 146).

Mushrooms and onions: Prepare as above with 1 small onion.
Spinach: Use 1 cup, chopped; steam in butter or mix with a little sour cream and garlic salt.
Asparagus: Use 3 or 4 stalks, steam in butter (or cooked leftovers) with Cream Sauce.
Cucumber: Use 1 medium. Scoop out seeds; stew in Cream Sauce.

NOTE
When using Cream Sauce, blend in just enough to make vegetables creamy and serve remainder over cooked omelette.

VARIATION
Roll omelette in grated Parmesan cheese. Place on buttered toast and sprinkle with more cheese. Put on a cookie sheet and place in hot (400°) oven for approximately two minutes, or until top is browned. Serve plain or with tomato sauce.

MENU SUGGESTION
Serve with Cold Fresh Cherry Soup (see page 43).

*Omelettes should be made in an omelette pan or a frying pan with rounded sides that is reserved for cooking omelettes only. The pan should never be washed, just wiped with a cloth or paper towel. If eggs begin to stick, "season" the pan as follows: Place on very high heat and sprinkle liberally with coarse salt; then remove from heat and, while it's still hot, wipe briskly with a clean cloth.

MIGUEL'S AUTHENTIC SPANISH OMELETTE

serving: 1
preparation time: 30 minutes

1 small potato, diced fine and salted
2 tablespoons oil (the Spanish always
    use olive oil)
½ small onion, diced fine
2 eggs, separated
    salt and pepper to taste

1. In a small frying pan, heat oil well and fry potato over medium heat until partially soft and golden, approximately 10 minutes. Drain and set aside.
2. In the same oil, fry onion until golden. Drain and set aside.
3. In a bowl, beat egg whites until foamy. Separately, beat yolks until pale yellow; combine whites and yolks.
4. Add potato, onion, and seasoning. Mix well.
5. Add a bit more oil to the same pan and heat over high heat. Pour mixture into pan and lower to medium heat. Tilt pan back and forth to distribute mixture evenly, and cook slowly until eggs are almost set and not runny.
6. Place a flat plate or pan cover over pan and flip omelette onto it. Then slide omelette back into pan and cook for a few minutes longer until slightly browned.
7. Remove from pan and serve hot or cold.

NOTE
A large omelette for several people can be made by increasing the above ingredients proportionately and cooking in a large frying pan; then cut into individual slices.

MENU SUGGESTION
Serve with Quick Cold Gazpacho (see page 45).

SHIRRED EGGS

serving: 1
preparation time: 15 minutes

1 teaspoon butter
2 eggs
1 slice tomato
1 slice Swiss or Cheddar cheese
1 teaspoon grated Parmesan cheese or
1 teaspoon heavy sweet cream
   salt to taste

1. Preheat oven to 375°
2. Spoon butter into a small casserole and place in oven until butter is melted.
3. Break eggs into a bowl, remove casserole from oven, and slide eggs carefully into casserole.
4. Place tomato, cheese, and grated cheese or cream on top and put back into oven.
5. Bake until whites have set. Season and serve hot.

VARIATION
Add a bit of cooked spinach or asparagus to tomato and cheese for a whole meal in one dish.

MENU SUGGESTION
Serve with Stuffed Tomatoes (see page 34).

CHEESE BLINTZES

yield: 10–12 blintzes
preparation time: 1 hour

BATTER:
   3 eggs, beaten lightly
   1 cup flour
1½ cups milk
   salt to taste

FILLING:
   1 pound cottage cheese
   1 pound farmer cheese
   2 egg yolks, beaten
   1 tablespoon butter or oil
   1 tablespoon lemon juice
   1 tablespoon lemon rind, grated
   3 tablespoons honey or maple syrup

1. Blend batter ingredients in a mixing bowl and set aside.
2. Lightly grease a small frying pan and warm over medium heat.
3. Pour in 1 ladleful of batter and tilt pan until batter covers bottom entirely. Allow a thin layer to adhere to bottom and quickly pour excess back into bowl. Cook "leaf" on one side only until it blisters, then flip onto plate, fried side up. Repeat process until all "leaves" are cooked. Keep pan lightly greased throughout.
4. Mix all filling ingredients in a bowl and put about 1 tablespoon of filling in center of each leaf. Fold all sides over each other and form into envelope shape.

5. Before serving, fry on both sides or bake in a medium oven until golden brown. Serve with sour cream, yoghurt, berry preserves, or fresh strawberries.

NOTE
Blintzes can be stored in freezer before frying. Fry without defrosting when ready.

VARIATION
A batter can be made with 1 egg by combining the following ingredients.

BATTER:
   1 egg
   1 cup milk
1½ cups flour
   4 tablespoons butter or oil
   1 cup water
   salt to taste

FILLING:
   Same as above.
   Follow directions above.

MENU SUGGESTION
This can be served for dessert, or as a main course for lunch or supper with Cold Quick "Real" Borscht (see page 41), or Cold Fresh Cherry Soup (see page 43).

BAKED CHEESE PANCAKES

yield: 8–10 pancakes
preparation time: 30 minutes

  1 pound farmer cheese
  ½ pound cream cheese
  ½ cup maple or rice syrup
  2 eggs
  1 teaspoon vanilla
  1 cup wheat germ or Grain Cereal (see
     page 180)

1. Preheat oven to 375°.
2. Mix cheeses with sugar, eggs, and
   vanilla until well blended.
3. Form mixture into small balls and
   flatten into ½-inch-thick pancakes.
4. Roll cakes in wheat germ or Grain
   Cereal and place on a greased cookie
   sheet.
5. Bake for 20 minutes. Serve hot—
   plain or with fresh crushed strawberries.

NOTE
Uncooked pancakes may be stored in
refrigerator for four or five days and
then baked as needed.

MENU SUGGESTION
Serve as a dessert or as a main dish for
lunch or supper with Cold Quick "Real"
Borscht (see page 41) or Cold Fresh Cherry Soup (see page 43).

NOODLES WITH CABBAGE

servings: 4–6
preparation time: 30 minutes

  1 pound broad noodles
  1 large onion, diced
  3 tablespoons butter or oil
  1 small cabbage, shredded
    salt and pepper to taste
  2 tablespoons poppy seeds
  2 tablespoons yoghurt
  1 tablespoon grated Parmesan cheese
      (optional)

1. Cook noodles in boiling salted water. Drain and set aside.
2. Sauté onion in 2 tablespoons butter or oil until golden.
3. Add cabbage and cook over low heat, stirring occasionally, until tender.
4. Add noodles and mix well with remaining butter or oil.
5. Mix in seasoning, poppy seeds, yoghurt and cheese. Cover and heat through. Serve hot.

MENU SUGGESTION
Serve with All-Green-Vegetable Soup (see page 49).

ITALIAN CHEESE AND POTATO PIE

servings: 4
preparation time: 1 hour

4 potatoes, peeled and cut in small
    chunks
½ cup light sweet cream or soymilk
2 tablespoons butter or oil
1 egg, separated
½ cup chopped parsley
    salt and pepper to taste
½ cup seasoned bread crumbs
½ pound Mozzarella cheese
½ cup grated Parmesan cheese

1. Preheat oven to 375°.
2. Boil potatoes, drain, and mash well
   with cream and butter or oil.
3. Beat egg yolk and mix with potatoes.
4. Whip egg white stiff with a pinch of
   salt and fold into potatoes with
   seasoning and parsley.
5. Grease a pie plate and sprinkle bottom liberally with bread crumbs.
   Then place potato mixture and
   sliced Mozzarella in alternate layers,
   starting with potatoes and finishing
   with cheese.
6. Sprinkle top with grated Parmesan
   cheese and dot with butter or oil.
7. Bake for approximately 45 minutes
   until top is golden brown. Serve hot.

MENU SUGGESTION
Serve with Fried Green Peppers (see page
84).

NOODLE PUDDING 1

servings: 4
preparation time: 1 hour

  ½ pound broad noodles
  2 tablespoons butter or oil
  3 eggs, separated
  ½ cup honey or ¾ cup rice syrup
  1 teaspoon cinnamon
  2 apples, sliced and sprinkled with lem-
     on juice
  ½ cup currants or raisins
  ½ cup chopped walnuts or toasted
     almonds
    salt to taste

1. Preheat oven to 350°.
2. Boil noodles in salted water for 15–20 minutes until cooked, yet firm.
3. Drain and run under cold water.
4. In a large frying pan, melt butter and toss noodles gently (try not to break them) until all butter is evenly distributed and absorbed.
5. Meanwhile, beat egg yolks and combine with other ingredients.
6. Remove noodles from heat and toss well with egg mixture.
7. Whip egg whites stiff and slowly fold in.
8. Turn into a greased casserole and bake for ½ hour. Serve hot or cold.

NOODLE PUDDING 2

servings: 4
preparation time: 1 hour

　½ pound broad noodles
　3 tablespoons butter, at room temper-
　　　ature or oil
　3 eggs, separated
　½ pound farmer cheese
　½ cup sour cream or yoghurt
　　　salt, pepper and paprika to taste

1. Preheat oven to 350°.
2. Prepare noodles as in Noodle Pudding 1 recipe, using 1 tablespoon
   butter.
3. Combine beaten egg yolks, cheese,
   sour cream, seasonings, and remaining butter. Add to noodles and toss
   well.
4. Whip egg whites stiff and fold in.
5. Turn into a greased casserole and
   bake for ½ hour. Serve hot.

VARIATION
Buttered bread crumbs sprinkled on bottom of casserole before adding noodles
and baking make this dish particularly
rich and delicious.

MENU SUGGESTION
Serve with Cream of Watercress Soup
(see page 51).

PASTA AND BEANS

servings: 4
preparation time: 40 minutes (not including soaking)

2 tablespoons each of olive oil and vegetable oil
1 onion, chopped
3 garlic cloves, minced
1 cup dried beans (such as navy, white, or chick peas), soaked 6 hours; or 1½ cups cooked beans
1 pound any small-size macaroni
½ eggplant or yellow squash, cooked and chopped (optional)
2 tomatoes, seeded and chopped
2 cups vegetable broth
1 teaspoon dried hot red pepper
salt and pepper to taste

1. Sauté onion and garlic in oil until brown.
2. If using dried beans, combine them with onion and garlic, cover with water, and cook until tender. If using cooked beans, use a small amount of liquid, combine with onions and garlic, and cook briefly over low heat.
3. Cook macaroni until parboiled. Drain.
4. Place macaroni, bean mixture and other vegetables in a large pot. Add vegetable broth and seasoning and cook over medium heat for about 10 minutes, or until macaroni is al dente. Serve hot.

VARIATIONS
For a stronger tomato flavor, add 1 tablespoon tomato paste to vegetables before final step. If you increase the amount of vegetable broth and serve in bowls, this dish becomes a soup.

MENU SUGGESTION
Serve with Grapefruit and Avocado Salad (see page 31).

66

C H A P T E R

4

Vegetables are the staple of the vegetarian diet. They provide a wealth of vitamins and minerals and can be prepared in a vast number of ways. Ideally, we should raise our own vegetables. Since this is impractical for many, the next best thing is to buy organically grown, preferably locally grown, vegetables. Don't be put off by some that may have a limp, shriveled appearance. Remember, these vegetables are free of preservatives, sprays and coloring. This may cause them to look "tired," but it's only be cause some of the water has evaporated. Buy them! They *do* taste better.

Most of the recipes that follow begin with fresh, well-scrubbed and unpeeled vegetables. The two cooking methods I use most often to prepare simple vegetables quickly and to best conserve their natural goodness are: STEAMING, using either a pressure cooker or vegetable steamer (see page 11). If you are using steamer, put no more than ½ inch water or unsalted vegetable broth in a heavy pot with a lid; bring to a boil; place vegetables in steamer; lower heat and cover tightly. Steam until vegetable is tender, but not mushy—what the Italians call "al dente," which, freely translated, means that you need teeth to eat it. Cooking time will vary with the vegetable (green beans take 15 minutes; beets, 30 minutes). QUICK-SAUTÉEING, which works best when vegetables are finely sliced or cut in strips. Heat a small amount of oil (1 tablespoon is usually enough) in a pan, add vegetables and cook for approximately 5 minutes over high heat. Lower heat to medium, cook another 10 minutes, stirring continuously; then add a little water, cover and simmer until tender. The amount of time and water will depend on the type and size of the vegetables being cooked. The addition of tamari sauce at the last minute enhances the taste of many quick-sautéed vegetables.

Avoid boiling vegetables except in soups, stews, and sauces. A good rule is to cook with as little water and in as short a time as possible.

In addition to the recipes in this chapter, you will find other vegetables and ways of preparing them on pages 15–20.

Vegetables

COLD TAHINI BROCCOLI

servings: 4
preparation time: 30 minutes (not including cooling)

    3 stalks broccoli
    2 lemons, sliced thin
    ½ cup tahini (sesame paste) thinned
        with about ¼ cup water
    3 garlic cloves, pressed
    4 tablespoons lemon juice
    1 tablespoon yoghurt
    ½ teaspoon (or more to taste) cayenne
        pepper
    dill or parsley, chopped

1. Wash broccoli and trim off bottom part of stalk and any other rough parts.
2. Place lemon slices on top and steam broccoli until tender. Then cool.
3. Meanwhile, make sauce by combining remaining ingredients, except for dill or parsley.
4. Arrange broccoli on serving dish, pour sauce all over and garnish with dill or parsley.

BRUSSELS SPROUTS, WATER CHESTNUTS, AND MUSHROOMS

servings: 4
preparation time: 30 minutes

    1 pound Brussels sprouts
    2 tablespoons butter or oil
    ½ pound mushrooms, sliced
    1 can (6 ounces) water chestnuts,
        drained
    1 teaspoon thyme
    ½ teaspoon ginger
    ½ cup pine nuts (optional)
      salt and pepper to taste

1. Steam sprouts until tender.
2. In a separate pan, sauté mushrooms, chestnuts, and pine nuts in butter or oil. Add seasoning, cover, and cook until mushrooms are tender.
3. Dish sprouts onto plate and carefully place mushroom mixture on top. Serve hot.

SAVOY CABBAGE AND POTATOES

servings: 4
preparation time: 45 minutes

1 Savoy cabbage, cut in small chunks
4 cups water
4 potatoes, peeled and diced fine
salt to taste
2 tablespoons oil
2 tablespoons flour
1 garlic clove, minced
pinch of pepper

1. Boil cabbage in salted water for approximately 10 minutes.
2. Add potatoes and boil vegetables together until potatoes are cooked. Drain, but reserve cooking water.
3. In a small frying pan, heat oil, add flour, and stir continuously until well browned. Add some cooking water and stir until smooth.
4. Combine cabbage, potatoes, browned flour, and at least 2 cups of cooking water. Add garlic and seasoning and mash all ingredients thoroughly. Mixture should be moist; add more water if necessary.
5. Heat through and serve hot.

MENU SUGGESTION
Serve with Honeyed Carrots (see page 74).

SWEET AND SOUR CABBAGE

servings: 4
preparation time: 20 minutes

   2 tablespoons butter or oil
   1 small cabbage, shredded
   1 egg
   2 tablespoons honey or rice syrup
   1 cup sour cream or yoghurt
   1 teaspoon prepared or freshly grated
     horseradish
     salt and pepper to taste
   2 tablespoons lemon juice

1. In a large frying pan, melt butter or heat oil.
2. Add cabbage and cook over low heat, stirring occasionally until tender, yet slightly crisp, approximately 10 minutes.
3. Meanwhile, beat egg slightly and mix in sweetener, sour cream or yoghurt, horseradish, salt, and pepper. Stir in lemon juice very slowly.
4. Pour sauce over cooked cabbage, heat through, and serve hot.

HONEYED CARROTS

servings: 4
preparation time: 20 minutes

4 carrots
2 tablespoons butter or oil
1 tablespoon honey
1 tablespoon toasted sesame seeds

1. Slice carrots horizontally about ¼ inch thick. Then cut pieces into thirds so that carrots resemble thin matchsticks.
2. In a frying pan, melt butter or heat oil, add carrots, and cover. Sauté approximately 5 minutes.
3. Add honey and sesame seeds, stir well, cover again, and sauté over low heat until tender—approximately 10 minutes.

CORN FRITTERS

servings: 4
preparation time: 20 minutes

> 2 eggs, separated
> salt and pepper to taste
> 2 cups cooked corn
> 3 tablespoons flour or meal or 2
>   tablespoons flour and 1
>   tablespoon wheat germ
> 3 tablespoons milk or soymilk or 3½
>   tablespoons heavy sweet cream
> ½ teaspoon vanilla
> ¼ cup vegetable oil
> honey

1. Beat egg yolks with a pinch of salt
   and combine with corn, flour or
   meal, milk, pepper, and vanilla.
2. Whip egg whites with a pinch of salt
   until stiff and fold into corn mixture.
3. In a deep frying pan, heat oil until
   hot. Drop mixture by tablespoonfuls
   and fry on both sides over high heat
   until crisp. Drain on paper towel.
   Serve immediately topped with honey.

GREEK STUFFED GRAPE LEAVES

servings: 4
preparation time: 2 hours

20 canned or bottled grape leaves (best
    quality)
½ cup rice
   water
1 large onion, diced fine
2 tablespoons butter or oil
1 teaspoon dill weed or fennel
1 tablespoon chopped fresh mint or 1
    teaspoon dried mint
   pinch of chili powder
   salt and pepper to taste
½ cup roasted chick peas (optional)
½ cup currants
½ cup pine nuts

1. Rinse grape leaves well in hot water
   to remove brine. Set aside.
2. Parboil rice in ½ cup water until
   water is absorbed.
3. Meanwhile, sauté onions in butter or
   oil until golden; then add rice and
   brown slightly. Add seasoning, chick
   peas, currants, and pine nuts. Remove from heat and allow to cool.
4. Place a teaspoonful of mixture in
   center of each grape leaf and roll

fairly tightly, starting at the stem
end and turning in the sides so that
filling is securely wrapped. Use all of
filling; any left over can be frozen.

5. Pack leaves into a pan, layer upon
   layer, and barely cover with water.
   Press a plate on top of leaves to prevent them from falling apart, and
   cover pan. Cook slowly for approximately 1½ hours—checking from
   time to time that some water re-
   mains on bottom of pan to prevent
   leaves from sticking or burning—
   until rice is cooked yet firm. Serve
   either hot or cold with a large bowl
   of yoghurt or sour cream.

NOTE
Any extra grape leaves may be stored in
a jar, covered with brine or water, and
kept in the refrigerator for future
stuffing.

MENU SUGGESTION
Serve with Cold Quick "Real" Borscht (see
page 41).

FRENCH GREEN BEANS WITH SUNFLOWER SEEDS

servings: 4
preparation time: 25 minutes

   1 pound green beans, tips removed
   2 tablespoons butter or oil
   ½ cup sunflower seeds
      salt and pepper to taste

1. Steam green beans until cooked yet firm.
2. In a large frying pan, melt butter over low heat, or heat oil.
3. Add beans, sunflower seeds, and seasoning. Increase to medium heat. Stir gently until beans are lightly browned. Serve immediately.

JERUSALEM ARTICHOKES

servings: 4
preparation time: 10 minutes

  2 tablespoons butter or oil
¼ cup water
  1 pound Jerusalem artichokes, sliced ¼
     inch thick
    salt and pepper to taste

1. Melt butter or heat oil and add water, artichokes, and seasoning.
2. Cover tightly and simmer until tender, yet crisp.
3. Serve with Cheese Sauce (see variation page 146).

LEEKS VINAIGRETTE

servings: 4
preparation time: 1½ hours

> 1 pound leeks, sliced lengthwise and
>   steamed
> 2 tablespoons olive oil
> 1 tablespoon vinegar or lemon juice
> 1 teaspoon mustard
> salt and pepper to taste

1. Allow leeks to cool at room temperature.
2. Combine remaining ingredients and pour over leeks.
3. Marinate for at least an hour; chill if possible.
4. Serve on lettuce as salad or as appetizer.

MUSHROOM PIE

yield: 1 large or 2 small pies
preparation time: 1¾ hours

CRUST
　2 cups pastry flour
　¼ teaspoon salt
　¼ pound butter or 3 tablespoons oil
　¼ cup (approximately) cold milk or
　　soymilk

FILLING
　1 pound mushrooms, sliced
　5 celery stalks, chopped
　1 small onion, chopped
　½ cup unsalted cashew nuts, chopped
　　pinch of thyme
　　salt and pepper to taste
　2 tablespoons butter or oil
　　Cream Sauce (page 146)

1. Sift pastry flour with salt.
2. Prepare pie crust by cutting butter or oil into flour first with two knives, then with fingers. Do not overmix; pastry dough should appear lumpy.
3. Add enough milk to hold dough together, blending mixture with a wooden spoon. Again: Do not overmix!
4. Divide dough into 2 balls (for a large pie) or into 4 balls (for 2 small pies). Chill pastry balls for approximately ½ hour.
5. While dough chills, prepare pie filling as follows: Sauté first 6 ingredients in 2 tablespoons butter or oil, cover, and cook over low heat until mushrooms are tender.
6. Meanwhile, in a separate pan, make Cream Sauce. Sauce should not be too thick; add more milk or cream if necessary.
7. Combine cooked mushroom mixture with Cream Sauce and blend well.
8. Preheat oven to 400°.
9. Roll out chilled dough balls on a floured board into circles approximately ¼ inch thick.
10. Grease a pie plate (or 2, if making small pies) and gently press 1 circle on bottom, reserving a strip of dough to place along edge of pie plate.
11. Pour in pie filling, then cover with another circle of dough. Fasten top layer of dough to bottom strip by pressing with fork tines. With a knife, make small slits evenly spaced around top layer to allow steam to escape while baking.
12. Reduce heat to 350° and bake in oven for ½ hours.
13. Allow to cool slightly before serving.

VARIATION
In place of mushrooms, substitute onions and grated Swiss (or cheddar) cheese; or green peas. The filling variations are many, and great joy can be derived from experimenting.

MUSHROOM CAPS BAKED IN CHEDDAR CHEESE SAUCE

servings: 4
preparation time: 30 minutes

    1 garlic clove, diced
    2 tablespoons butter or oil
    1 pound mushrooms, caps only
      salt and pepper to taste
      dash of Worcestershire sauce
      Cheese Sauce (see page 146), double
        recipe
      pinch of cayenne

1. Preheat oven to 350°
2. Sauté garlic lightly in butter or oil until soft; then discard garlic.
3. Add mushroom caps and seasoning and cook over low heat, covered, until tender.
4. Prepare a double recipe of Cheese Sauce, using Cheddar cheese and adding cayenne.
5. Transfer mushroom caps to a greased casserole, cover with sauce, and place in oven for a few minutes until top is lightly browned and bubbly. Serve hot.

SOUR CREAM MUSHROOMS

servings: 4
preparation time: 10 minutes

1 pound mushrooms
1 small onion, diced
2 tablespoons butter or oil
    salt and pepper to taste
2 tablespoons white wine
2 tablespoons sherry
¾ cup sour cream or yoghurt
1 tablespoon minced chives
3 tablespoons diced cucumber

82

1. Leave small mushrooms whole; cut large ones in half.
2. Sauté mushrooms and onion in butter or oil for approximately 5 minutes.
3. Add seasoning and wine and cook over low heat for 1 minute longer.
4. Add sour cream or yoghurt, chives, and cucumbers. Mix thoroughly and heat. Serve hot.

MENU SUGGESTION
Serve with buttered noodles or Noodles with Cabbage (see page 63).

INDIAN PAKORA

servings: 4–6
preparation time: approximately 30
    minutes

BATTER
   2 cups chick-pea flour
   1 teaspoon cumin
   1 teaspoon coriander
   ½ teaspoon cayenne
     salt to taste
     water, very cold

VEGETABLES (use no more than four varieties at one meal):
     carrots, sliced in ½-inch-wide, 1-inch-
      long strips
     cauliflower, broken into small
      flowerets
     eggplant, sliced horizontally, ½ inch
      wide
     green pepper, sliced in ½-inch-wide
      strips
     potatoes, sliced very thin
     spinach, coarsely chopped
     zucchini, sliced horizontally, ½ inch
      wide

   oil
   tamari sauce

1. Prepare batter by blending all ingredients thoroughly.
2. Choose vegetables. Dip into batter and
   coat well.
3. Pour at least two inches of oil into a
   large frying pan, and fry vegetables,
   one variety at a time, until golden
   brown. (*Note:* Oil must be *very* hot—
   test by dropping in a bit of batter.
   When batter bubbles on contact, oil is
   ready.) Cooking time will vary; carrots,
   eggplant, and potatoes take longest.
4. Drain on paper towel and serve as
   quickly as possible with tamari sauce
   on the side.

VARIATION
This dish is delicious accompanied by a
bowl of sauce made with two cups of
sour cream or yoghurt flavored with 1
minced garlic clove and salt to taste.

MENU SUGGESTION
Serve with plain rice or Farina Side Dish
(see page 102).

FRIED GREEN PEPPERS

servings: 4–6
preparation time: 15 minutes

6 large or 12 small green peppers
  salt to taste
4 garlic cloves, whole
¼ cup olive oil

1. Remove stem and seeds from peppers
   in the following manner: Push in stem
   until it feels loose, then quickly pull
   out stem with seeds. Cut large peppers in quarters, small peppers in
   halves, lengthwise. Season.
2. In a large frying pan, brown garlic in
   hot oil.
3. Over medium heat, fry peppers until
   tender and well browned.
4. Drain on paper towel and serve immediately.

NOTE
For a decorative splash, after step 3 add
pimientos or cooked sweet red peppers
and heat through.

TOP-OF-THE-STOVE POTATO PUDDING

servings: 4
preparation time: 40 minutes

   1 pound potatoes, peeled and grated
   1 onion, grated
   2 eggs, beaten
     salt and pepper to taste
   2 tablespoons flour or meal
 ¼ cup oil
  1 onion, sliced thin
 ½ cup chopped parsley

1. Mix potatoes and grated onion together.
2. Add eggs, seasoning, and flour or meal. Mixture should pour easily but not be too liquid—add more flour if necessary.
3. In a large deep frying pan, heat oil and brown sliced onion and parsley.
4. Pour in potato mixture, reduce to medium heat, and cook for approximately 15 minutes, or until top is not runny, and bottom is crisply browned.
5. Take pan to the sink and cover with a large plate. Flip pan over and then slide pudding back into pan, cooked side up. Return to heat and continue cooking until bottom is browned and potatoes are thoroughly cooked.
6. Serve hot with or without Brown Sauce (see page 147).

MENU SUGGESTION
Serve with Oriental Spinach (see page 89).

POTATO PANCAKES (LATKES)

yield: about 20 pancakes
preparation time: 30 minutes

  1 large onion, sliced thin
    oil
  6 large potatoes, peeled and grated
  4 heaping tablespoons pancake flour
  2 eggs, slightly beaten
  1 onion, grated
    salt and pepper to taste

1. Fry onion slices lightly in hot oil.
2. Mix remaining ingredients well.
3. For each pancake spoon 1 heaping tablespoon of batter into oil, flattening pancake with a spoon immediately.
4. Fry for approximately 5 minutes on each side, or until brown and crispy.
5. Drain on paper towel and serve hot.

VEGETARIAN SHISHKEBAB

servings: 4–6
preparation time: 3 hours

MARINADE
  ½ cup tamari sauce
  ¼ cup water
  1 tablespoon curry powder
  1 teaspoon ginger
  1 bay leaf
  1 onion, sliced thin
  2 garlic cloves, minced
    Pinch each of salt and pepper

VEGETABLES
  5 large tomatoes, cubed; or 20 cherry
    tomatoes
  4 green peppers, seeds removed and
    cubed
  2 large onions, cut in small chunks; or
    12 whole small white onions
  ½ pound mushrooms, caps only

1. Blend all marinade ingredients well.
2. Place vegetables in a deep bowl and
   cover with marinade. If more liquid is
   required, increase tamari sauce and
   water proportionately.
3. Cover bowl and leave in a cool
   place—do not refrigerate—for at
   least 2 hours.
4. Remove vegetables from marinade
   and place alternately on skewers.
   Broil or barbecue, basting with
   marinade, until vegetables are
   tender and well browned. Serve hot
   over rice.

SPINACH DUMPLINGS

servings: 4
preparation time: at least 2¼ hours

- 1 pound spinach, chopped
- 2 eggs, beaten
  pinch each of oregano and sage
  salt to taste
  flour
- 2 cups croutons, browned in butter or
  oil
- 2 tablespoons oil

1. Steam spinach until tender and drain well.
2. Combine spinach with remaining ingredients, using just enough flour to give mixture a soft, biscuit-like texture.
3. Cover mixture and chill for at least 2 hours.
4. When ready to serve, wet hands and form mixture into small balls. Boil in salted water for 10–15 minutes.
5. Serve hot in Tomato Sauce (see page 154) or bake briefly in oven.

VARIATION
Sauté spinach dumplings in mixture of 2 tablespoons oil and 1 tablespoon minced garlic clove until browned. Drain and serve.

MENU SUGGESTION
Serve with Sweet Cream of Carrot Soup (see page 42).

ORIENTAL SPINACH

servings: 4
preparation time: 15 minutes

2 tablespoons sesame oil
2 garlic cloves, minced
1 pound spinach, torn
   teaspoon salt or tamari sauce
   crushed red pepper (optional)

1. In a large deep frying pan brown
   garlic in hot oil.
2. Add spinach and toss well so that oil
   is evenly distributed.
3. Add seasoning, toss again, and cook
   over medium heat. Stir frequently
   and cook until spinach is tender but
   not soggy, approximately five
   minutes. Serve immediately.

BAKED SQUASH

servings: 6–8
preparation time: 1½ hours

   2 pounds any "hard" winter squash,
      such as butternut, acorn or
      Hubbard
      tamari sauce, to taste
   3 tablespoons oil
   1 cup chopped roasted nuts, pumpkin
      or sunflower seeds
  ½ cup water

1. Scrub squash, clean, and slice like a melon into fourths, sixths, or whatever is a convenient size.
2. Grease the outside of the squash and amply grease the baking tray(s).
3. Place the squash slices in the tray(s), sprinkle with the chopped nuts or seeds, and sprinkle liberally with tamari.
4. Pour water into bottom of tray(s), cover, and bake in 375-degree oven for about an hour or until tender. Remove cover for last 10 minutes of baking. Squash should be tender but not dried out.

SQUASH PANCAKES

yield: 6–8
preparation time: 25 minutes

1 large butternut or winter squash,
   peeled and grated
2 heaping tablespoons flour
2 eggs
   salt and pepper to taste
   oil

1. Mix all ingredients, except oil,
   together.
2. Wet hands. Roll batter into balls and
   flatten into cakes.
3. Carefully place each pancake into
   hot, deep oil.
4. Fry on medium heat for about 10
   minutes on each side.
5. Place on paper towels to drain and
   serve hot.

MENU SUGGESTION
Serve with Fresh Asparagus Soup (see
page 40).

JAPANESE TEMPURA

servings: 4–6
preparation time: 30 minutes

BATTER
  1 cup flour
  2 eggs, beaten
  ½ cup water, very cold
  ¼ cup tamari sauce

VEGETABLES (use no more than four varieties at one meal)
  broccoli, broken into small flowerets
  carrots, sliced into ½-inch-wide, 1-inch-long strips
  cauliflower, broken into small flowerets
  eggplant, sliced horizontally, ½ inch wide
  green pepper, sliced in ½-inch-wide strips
  mushroom caps, whole
  onions, sliced in ½-inch-wide rings
  zucchini, sliced horizontally, ½ inch wide

  vegetable oil
  tamari sauce

1. Prepare batter by blending all ingredients thoroughly.
2. Choose vegetables. Dip into batter and coat well.
3. Pour at least three inches of oil in a large frying pan and fry vegetables, one variety at a time, until golden brown. (*Note:* Oil must be *very* hot—test by dropping in a bit of batter. When batter bubbles on contact, oil is ready.) Cooking time will vary; carrots, eggplant, and mushrooms take longest.
4. Drain on paper towel and serve as quickly as possible with tamari sauce on the side.

NOTE
Leftover batter can be dropped by spoonfuls into oil, fried, and eaten like popovers, or stored in refrigerator for future use.

MENU SUGGESTION
Serve with plain rice and Cucumber and Yoghurt Salad (see page 29).

ARABIAN-STYLE VEGETABLES

servings: 4
preparation time: 30 minutes

    2 tablespoons oil
    1 large onion, sliced thin
    2 garlic cloves, minced
    1 tomato, peeled and diced
    1 small cauliflower, broken into
        flowerets
    ½ pound string beans, snapped in half
    2 potatoes, peeled and diced small
    salt and pepper to taste

1. Heat oil in a deep frying pan, and sauté onions and garlic until golden.
2. Add tomato and sauté until tender.
3. Add remaining vegetables, seasoning, and a little water.
4. Cover and simmer until vegetables are tender. If mixture begins to dry out, add more water. Serve hot.

1 large eggplant (or vegetable of your
   choice; see VARIATIONS)
   melted butter or oil
4–6 tablespoons bread crumbs
   grated Parmesan or Cheddar cheese
   (optional)

STUFFING
   2 small onions, chopped fine
   2 garlic cloves, minced
   2 celery stalks, chopped fine
   2 tablespoons chopped parsley
   2 tablespoons butter or oil
   1 cup bread crumbs or cooked rice
   salt and pepper to taste

1. Steam eggplant until almost tender.
   Cut in half and remove pulp. Chop
   pulp and set aside to be used in
   stuffing.
2. Preheat oven to 350°.
3. Sauté onions, garlic celery, and parsley in 2 tablespoons butter or oil for
   approximately 5 minutes.

servings: 4
preparation time: varies with vegetable

4. Add remaining stuffing ingredients
   and chopped eggplant pulp and mix
   well.
5. Fill center of each eggplant half with
   stuffing. Top with bread crumbs and
   brush surface with melted butter or
   oil. Sprinkle with cheese (if desired).
6. Place stuffed eggplant halves in a
   casserole with approximately ¼ inch
   of water on bottom. Bake until
   brown and tender.

VARIATIONS
In place of eggplant, any one of the fol-
lowing vegetables can be used as
described below:
ARTICHOKES (1 medium per serving):
Steam until tender. Remove stems, bot-
tom leaves, and about ¼ inch off tops.
Chop stems and set aside for stuffing.
Spread leaves apart and remove thistle.
Fill center and rows between leaves with
stuffing. Stuffing variation: Add capers
and ¼ cup grated Parmesan cheese.

CAULIFLOWER (1 large): Steam until tender. Remove center stalk; chop and set aside for stuffing. Stuffing variation: Add tamari sauce, a dash of Tabasco sauce, and chopped toasted almonds.
PEPPERS (1 medium per serving): Cut slice from top and remove seeds. Steam until tender. Chop tops and set aside for stuffing. Stuffing variation: Substitute corn kernels for rice or bread crumbs, omit onions and celery, and add 2 cups grated Cheddar cheese. Mix 1 tablespoon flour with 2 tablespoons milk and a pinch of cayenne and combine with rest of ingredients.
ZUCCHINI (1 medium per serving): Follow directions for eggplant. Stuffing variations: Add oregano, pine nuts and ½ cup grated cheese; or raisins and chopped mint; or chopped tomatoes and cabbage leaves (cooked and chopped).
MENU SUGGESTION
Serve with lettuce salad with French Dressing (see page 157).

EASY VEGETABLE SUKIYAKI

servings: 4–6
preparation time: 20 minutes

1 pound mushrooms, sliced
2 tablespoons oil
1 pound spinach, chopped
3 celery stalks, diced
2 cups bean sprouts
1 can (6 ounces) bamboo shoots
¼ cup tamari sauce
2 tablespoons Chinese brown sauce or molasses
¼ cup vegetable broth
salt and pepper to taste
1 tablespoon sherry (optional)

1. In a large deep frying pan or wok, heat oil and brown mushrooms.
2. Add remaining ingredients, stir well, and cook over medium heat for approximately 10 minutes or until vegetables are tender yet slightly crisp. Serve immediately.

MENU SUGGESTION
Serve with Chinese Style Fried Rice (see page 106).

VEGETARIAN EGG ROLLS

yield: 16–20 egg rolls
preparation time: 30 minutes

WRAPPING
    2 cups pastry flour
    2 eggs
  2¾ cups water

FILLING
    2 tablespoons oil
    2 tablespoons tamari sauce
    3 scallions, sliced fine
    2 cups shredded bean sprouts
    2 cups shredded cabbage
   ½ cup toasted sesame seeds
     salt to taste
     cornstarch
     water
     oil

1. Beat wrapping ingredients together until smooth.
2. Lightly grease a small frying pan. Pour in 1 ladleful of batter and tilt pan until batter covers bottom entirely. Allow a thin layer to adhere to bottom and quickly pour excess back into bowl. Cook on one side for approximately 1 minute. Flip onto a plate, fried side up. Repeat process until all batter is used.
3. In a large pan, heat oil and tamari sauce. Add remaining filling ingredients and stir well until tender yet crisp, approximately 3 minutes.
4. Place approximately 2 tablespoons of filling on lower half of wrapping, fold in sides, and roll tightly. Make a paste with a little cornstarch and water; brush along ends, press, and seal. Continue until all filling is used.
5. In hot oil, fry egg rolls until well browned on all sides. Drain on paper towels. Serve hot or cold.

NOTE
Any leftover wrappings can be fried and eaten like potato chips.

CHILLED ZUCCHINI

servings: 4
preparation time: 20 minutes
    (not including chilling)

    4 small zucchini, sliced diagonally, ¼
        inch thick
    1 tablespoon chopped fresh mint or 1
        tablespoon dried mint
    2 tablespoons chopped fresh dill or
    1 tablespoon dill weed
    ⅓ cup olive oil

1. Combine zucchini with herbs and
    sauté in oil until tender and golden.
2. Allow to cool, chill, and serve with
    lots of plain yoghurt.

CHAPTER

5

Rice, whole grains and beans are all marvelous sources of energy and can be served frequently as filling main courses.

The rice you use should be brown rice, either short- or long-grain. White rice, because of the polishing and processing it undergoes, lacks flavor and food value (and is also more fattening!). Brown rice is simple to cook; the main difference is that it takes a little longer. Here are two basic ways to cook it:

Boiled. Put one part rice in a strainer or colander and wash thoroughly with cold water. Place rice in a heavy pot with two parts water and some salt. Bring water to a boil and boil rapidly until water is absorbed to about ½ inch above rice. Cover tightly, lower heat and cook slowly for at least 45 minutes or until rice is tender, yet firm. Add more water if necessary.

Sauteed and steamed. Heat a small amount of oil or butter in a heavy pot, sauté one part rice lightly, stirring constantly, until toasted. Add two parts boiling water, cover tightly, lower heat and cook slowly for at least 45 minutes or until rice is tender, yet firm. Add more water if necessary.

Note: Onions, mushrooms, or other vegetables may be sautéed and steamed together with the rice.

A wide range of menus is made possible by the variety of whole grains available. In many recipes, the grains specified can be interchanged with rice or another grain. Some of the grains most commonly used are bulgur, barley (hulled and unpearled), millet, buckwheat groats (kasha) and wheat berry (wheat grain, green corn).

A basic way to cook most grains is the same sautéeing-and-steaming method used for rice. *Important:* Never stir rice or grains once the water is boiling, as this will cause them to stick.

Dried beans and peas are delicious and versatile either alone or with rice or grains. There are many different kinds: lima (large and baby), navy, marrow, small white, pinto, kidney, lentil, soybeans; split peas (green and yellow), black-eyed peas, chick peas (ceci, garbanzos), etc.

Most dried beans need at least 6 hours to soak and at least double in volume when soaked; 2 cups of dried beans will generally serve 6 people. Soaked beans may be stored in the refrigerator for later use.

Never cook beans with salt; it tends to toughen them. The addition of a few strips of seaweed, such as *wakame* or *kombu* (available in natural food and Oriental stores) not only enhances the flavor, but helps reduce the flatulence often associated with beans. Simply soak the seaweed for a few minutes to soften it, rinse thoroughly and add to beans prior to cooking. Because seaweed is naturally salty, beans will need less additional seasoning.

When puréeing beans, do so while they are still warm and use some of the cooking liquid.

Vegetable broth may be substituted for water in all rice, grain and bean recipes.

Yoghurt is a delicious accompaniment to many grain and bean dishes.

Grains, Rice, and Beans

BAKED BARLEY AND MUSHROOMS

servings: 4
preparation time: 1½ hours

1 garlic clove, diced
1 onion, diced
½ pound mushrooms, sliced
1 cup barley
   salt or tamari sauce and pepper to
     taste
2 tablespoons butter or oil
2½ cups vegetable broth, boiling

1. Preheat oven to 350°
2. In a large deep frying pan, sauté garlic, onion, mushrooms, barley, and seasoning in butter or oil. Stir frequently until barley is lightly browned.
3. Place in a casserole and stir in broth.
4. Cover and bake for approximately 1 hour. If barley is too firm when all the liquid is absorbed, add additional boiling water. However, avoid overcooking—barley is more delicious when firm and slightly crunchy.

NOTE
Be very careful when removing cover from casserole, as steam builds up within.

MENU SUGGESTION
Serve with All-Green-Vegetable Soup (see page 49).

COUSCOUS WITH VEGETABLES

servings: 4
preparation time: 2 hours
(not including soaking)

1 cup chick peas, soaked 6 hours, or 2 cups cooked chick peas
1 pound couscous (a wheat cereal resembling semolina which can be purchased boxed or loose in Near Eastern shops, natural food stores, and most supermarkets)
1 pound yellow or butternut squash or pumpkin, cut in chunks
3 green peppers, cut in quarters
1 turnip, cut in chunks
2 celery stalks, cut in chunks
1 onion, cut in chunks
3 tomatoes, cut in chunks (optional)
1 teaspoon salt
1 teaspoon paprika (sharp)
1 pinch of cumin seed
2 cloves

GARNISH (optional)
6 onions or leeks, sliced
Oil
½ cup blanched almonds
½ cup raisins
pinch of saffron powder
1 teaspoon cinnamon

1. If using soaked chick peas, drain, reserve liquid, and boil over low heat until tender, approximately 1 hour.
2. Put couscous in a bowl, pour some hot water over it, and allow to stand for 10 minutes until water is absorbed.
3. Using a special couscous pot (see NOTE) pour into lower pot the reserved water from chick peas—or liquid from canned cooked chick peas—and additional water to make 3 quarts altogether. Bring to a boil.
4. Place vegetables, chick peas, and seasoning in boiling water; put couscous in upper pot, cover, and steam for 15 minutes.
5. Meanwhile, make garnish, if desired, by browning onions in oil, adding remaining ingredients and cooking, covered, for 15 minutes.
6. Transfer couscous to a bowl, add two ladlefuls of cooking liquid, and stir well.
7. Return couscous to upper pot, cover, and steam for another 15 minutes.
8. Place couscous on a platter, spoon vegetables on top, and pour liquid from lower pot over them. Serve with the bowl of onion garnish.

NOTE
A couscous pot is a double pot. The upper pot is perforated and fits into the lower pot—much like a double-boiler—but the perforations allow the steam to come through to cook and flavor the couscous. It might be possible to improvise a similar kind of pot, but the actual couscous pot is best to use for this dish.

FARINA SIDE DISH

servings: 4
preparation time: 30 minutes

   2 potatoes, peeled and diced small
   1 cup water
   ¼ cup oil
   2 cups farina
     salt and pepper to taste

1. Boil potatoes in salted water.
2. Meanwhile, heat oil, add farina, and
   sauté over low heat. Stir constantly
   until farina is golden brown.
3. Mash potatoes in cooking water and
   add seasoning.
4. Add sautéed farina to mashed potatoes. Mix well, cover, and cook over
   low heat until farina is tender. Serve
   hot.

NOTE
When finished, this dish should resemble
fine egg barley.

BUCKWHEAT GROATS (KASHA) WITH MUSHROOM SAUCE

servings: 4–6
preparation time: 30 minutes

1 small onion, chopped fine
2 tablespoons oil
2 cups buckwheat groats
1 egg, beaten well
  salt and pepper to taste
  vegetable broth, boiling

SAUCE ½ pound mushrooms, sliced
  1 tablespoon butter or oil
    Brown Sauce (see page 147), double
      recipe; or Special Brown Sauce (see
      page 148)

1. In a large pot, sauté onion lightly in oil.
2. Mix groats and egg together well. Add salt and pepper.
3. Toast groats mixture in oil, stirring constantly with a wooden spoon un-til groats are browned, separated, and dry.
4. Gradually add vegetable broth to approximately ½ inch above groats. Lower heat, cover, and cook until broth is absorbed. If groats are too firm, add more broth or boiling water.
5. In a small pan, sauté mushrooms in butter or oil until tender. Combine Brown Sauce (made with onion) with cooked mushrooms and mix well with groats. Heat through and serve hot.

MENU SUGGESTION
Serve with asparagus with Green Sauce (see page 153).

WHEAT BERRY
IN HAZELNUT-LEEK SAUCE

servings: 4–6
preparation time: 1 hour

2 cups wheat berry
2 tablespoons oil
water
½ cup chopped hazelnuts
3 garlic cloves, minced
2 leeks, cut in ½-inch pieces
salt to taste

1. In a large frying pan, toast grain in 1 tablespoon oil, moving pan constantly, until grain begins to pop.
2. Add water to a level approximately 1 inch above grain and boil over low heat, uncovered, for approximately 45 minutes, or until tender. Add more boiling water if necessary.
3. Meanwhile, sauté nuts, garlic, leeks, and salt in remaining oil. Add about 1 tablespoon water, cover tightly and steam over low heat for approximately 20 minutes, or until water is absorbed.
4. When grain is tender, transfer to a casserole, spoon nut-leek sauce on top, and cover. Steam in a warm (300°) oven for approximately 15 minutes before serving.

NOTE
As grains vary, test to see if more water is needed. When cooked, grain should be firm and slightly crunchy.

MENU SUGGESTION
Serve with Many-Vegetable Salad (see page 36).

BAKED RICE AND VEGETABLES

servings: 4–6
preparation time: 2 hours

2 cups rice
2 tablespoons oil
4 carrots or 1 yellow squash, cut in
    chunks
6 small whole onions or 2 large onions,
    cut in chunks
½ cabbage, 2 turnips, or 2 white radish-
    es cut in chunks
3 garlic cloves, chopped
2 tablespoons tamari sauce
water

1. In a large heavy pot, toast rice in oil until lightly browned, stirring constantly with a wooden spoon.
2. Place vegetables over rice.
3. Combine water and tamari sauce. Pour to a level approximately 1 inch above vegetables.
4. Tightly cover pot and bake in 350° oven for approximately 1½ hours, or until water is absorbed. If rice is too firm, add more water, cover, and continue baking until tender. Serve hot.

VARIATION
Barley, kasha, or wheat berry can be substituted for the rice. Adjust amount of water to the type of grain used.

CHINESE-STYLE FRIED RICE

servings: 2
preparation time: 10 minutes

    2 tablespoons oil
    2 scallions, diced
    1 celery stalk, diced
    2 cups rice, cooked
    2 eggs
    4 tablespoons milk, soymilk, or vegeta-
        ble broth
    1 tablespoon tamari sauce
      pinch of nutmeg
    2 tablespoons chopped parsley

1. In a large frying pan or wok, heat oil. Sauté scallions and celery until golden.
2. Add rice, stirring constantly with a wooden spoon, and fry for approximately 5 minutes.
3. Beat egg with milk, tamari sauce, and seasoning.
4. Pour egg mixture into rice and stir over medium heat until eggs set. Serve hot.

NOTE
This dish is enhanced if left in a warm oven for a few minutes before serving.

CUBAN RICE

servings: 4–6
preparation time: 1 hour

  2 cups rice
  4 onions
  ¼ cup olive oil
  4 garlic cloves, minced
  3 green peppers, sliced
  5 tomatoes, peeled, seeded, and cubed
  1 teaspoon oregano
  ½ teaspoon crushed, hot red pepper
     (optional)
    salt and pepper to taste
  ½ pound mushrooms, sliced

1. Cook rice until tender.
2. Meanwhile, in a large frying pan, sauté onions in oil until golden.
3. Add garlic and brown slightly.
4. Add peppers, tomatoes, and seasoning; reduce heat, cover, and simmer.
5. In a separate pan, sauté mushrooms in a little oil.
6. When all vegetables are tender, combine them. Serve hot over rice.

FANCY PERSIAN RICE

servings: 6–8
preparation time: 1½ hours

> 4 cups long-grain rice
> 3 potatoes, peeled and sliced thin
> ⅓ cup raisins or ½ cup currants,
>   soaked in water and drained
> ⅛ teaspoon saffron, soaked in ¼ cup
>   hot water
> 3 tablespoons butter or oil
>   salt to taste

1. Rinse rice and boil in salted water. When tender but still firm, rinse again in cold water to separate grains.
2. Preheat oven to 350°.
3. Grease bottom of casserole and cover with raw potato slices. Dot with lumps of butter or oil and spread rice evenly on top. Sprinkle with raisins or currants and saffron water.
4. Melt remaining butter or oil and pour over rice.
5. Cover and steam in oven for approximately 15 minutes.
6. Remove from oven, shake gently from side to side, and allow to stand, uncovered, for 10 minutes.
7. Transfer to serving dish and discard potatoes. Serve warm.

MENU SUGGESTION
Serve with a large bowl of stewed prunes or plums, and lettuce salad with Miso and Tahini Sauce (see page 149).

VEGETABLE PAELLA

servings: 4
preparation time: 1 hour

2 cups rice
5 cups water
2 onions, sliced fine
4 garlic cloves, minced
2 large or 4 small green peppers, sliced
   thin
1 large tomato, sliced
3 tablespoons olive oil
1 bay leaf
1 teaspoon powdered saffron
salt to taste
1 cup peas, cooked
4 pimientos, diced

1. Boil rice in 2½ cups salted water, covered, until water is absorbed.
2. Meanwhile, in a large pot, brown onions, garlic, peppers, and tomato in oil.
3. Mix rice with vegetables and add remaining water and seasoning. Cover and cook over low heat until water is nearly absorbed.
4. Add peas and pimientos. Do not stir. Check to see if rice is tender—if necessary add boiling water. Serve hot.

MENU SUGGESTION
Serve with spinach salad and Tahini Dressing (see page 155).

DRIED BEANS WITH GARLIC SAUCE

servings: 4
preparation time: 1½ hours (not including soaking)

1 pound white or black beans, soaked
    6 hours
1 head garlic, whole
1 garlic clove, minced
½ cup olive oil
1 teaspoon cumin
1 tablespoon salt

1. Peel outer covering of garlic but leave cluster whole.
2. Cover beans and garlic with water and cook, uncovered, until beans are almost tender.
3. Drain and remove garlic. Place beans in a bean pot or suitable pan.
4. In a small frying pan, sauté minced garlic clove in oil until yellow. Strain and combine oil with cumin and salt.
5. Pour oil mixture onto beans and cook, uncovered, for approximately 25 minutes. Serve hot.

MENU SUGGESTION
Serve with Farina Side Dish (see page 102).

"HOT" BEANS AND SPINACH

servings: 6
preparation time: 45 minutes (not includ-
    ing soaking)

    2 cups dried white or pinto beans,
        soaked 6 hours
    2 tablespoons vegetable oil
    2 garlic cloves, minced
    1 pound spinach, chopped
    1 hot red pepper, diced
      salt and pepper to taste
      pinch of cayenne

    1. Cook beans over low heat until
       tender. Reserve 1 cup cooking liquid
       before draining.
    2. In a deep frying pan, sauté garlic in
       oil.
    3. Add spinach and stir for approxi-
       mately 5 minutes.
    4. Add beans, red pepper, and season-
       ing. Stir thoroughly over high heat
       until beans are lightly browned.
       Then add cooking water, lower heat,
       cover, and cook for approximately 20
       minutes, until all flavors are well
       blended. Serve hot.

NOTE
This dish should be saucelike, so add a bit
more water if beans begin to dry out
during cooking.

MENU SUGGESTION
Serve with rice with Tamari and Tahini
Sauce (see page 150).

BULENT'S CHICK PEAS

servings: 4
preparation time: 30 minutes (not including soaking)

2 small onions, diced
1 tomato, peeled, seeded, and diced
2 tablespoons olive oil
1 cup dried chick peas, soaked 6 hours
    pinch each of thyme, basil, oregano,
        and salt

1. Cook chick peas until almost tender.
2. Sauté onions and tomato in olive oil until tender.
3. Add chick peas and herbs. Cover and sauté over low heat until chick peas are tender.

MENU SUGGESTION
Serve with rice cooked with pine nuts and Chilled Zucchini (see page 71).

HOT LENTIL PÂTE

servings: 4
preparation time: 1½ hours

1½ cups lentils
2 tablespoons oil
2 small onions, diced
1 garlic clove, minced
½ cup chopped parsley
2 small hard rolls or 3 slices hard
    bread, soaked in water
    pinch each of thyme, coriander,
      celery seed, and chili powder
2 tablespoons chopped fresh dill or 1
    tablespoon dill weed
    salt and pepper to taste
1 egg, beaten
    juice of ½ lemon
    dash of tamari sauce

1. Wash lentils well and boil slowly for approximately 40 minutes, or until tender.
2. Meanwhile, sauté onions, garlic, and parsley in oil. Squeeze out excess water from rolls or bread and add to onion mixture. Add seasoning. Stir well over medium heat for 10 minutes, adding water if necessary (mixture should be fairly moist).
3. Preheat oven to 350°.
4. Mash lentils in a food mill or blender.
5. Combine lentils with onion mixture, egg, lemon juice, and tamari sauce; mix well. Mixture should have a heavy consistency.
6. Bake in a greased pan for 30 minutes, or until bottom is well browned. Serve hot or cold.

113

MENU SUGGESTION
Serve with Brussels Sprouts, Water Chestnuts, and Mushrooms (see page 97).

MIDDLE EASTERN LIMA BEANS

servings: 6
preparation time: 2½ hours (not including soaking)

2 cups dried lima beans, soaked 6
    hours
8 cups salted water
2 tablespoons butter or oil
2 onions, chopped
¼ teaspoon turmeric
½ teaspoon powdered cloves
    salt and pepper to taste
1 large tart apple, cored and chopped

1. Drain beans, place in a large pot, and
   cover with salted water. Boil until
   tender, approximately 1½–2 hours.
2. Drain, but reserve cooking water.
3. In a large frying pan or pot, heat
   butter or oil and sauté onions until
   golden. Add seasoning and apple. Stir
   well and simmer until apple is
   cooked.
4. Add cooked beans and enough of
   the cooking water to moisten. Cook
   slowly for 8–10 minutes. Serve hot.

MENU SUGGESTION
Serve with rice, bulgur, or millet in Brown
Sauce (with mushrooms) (see page 147).

BAKED SOYBURGERS

servings: 8
preparation time: 45 minutes (not including soaking beans)

  2 onions, chopped
  ⅛ pound mushrooms, sliced
  2 tablespoons butter or oil
  4 slices stale bread, cut into croutons
  2 garlic cloves, pressed
  ½ pound soybeans, soaked at least 8
      hours and cooked
  4 ounces nuts, preferably cashews and
      peanuts, roasted
  1 teaspoon sage
  1 teaspoon thyme
  3 tablespoons miso
  2 cups brown sauce (see page 147)

1. Saute onions and mushrooms until
   golden in butter or oil.
2. Saute croutons and garlic in remaining butter or oil until brown.
3. Combine soybeans, onions, nuts,
   seeds, croutons and seasoning, and
   form into patties.
4. Combine miso and brown sauce
5. Place in baking pan and cover with
   sauce. Bake in moderate oven until
   well done.

SOYBEANS AND MUSHROOMS

servings: 4
preparation time: 25 minutes

½ onion, diced
1 garlic clove, minced
2 tablespoons butter or oil
½ pound mushrooms, sliced
    salt and pepper to taste
1 tablespoon tamari sauce
1 tablespoon molasses or Chinese
    brown sauce
2 cups soybeans, cooked
1 tablespoon chopped fresh dill or 1
    teaspoon dill weed

1. Sauté onion and garlic in butter or oil until golden.
2. Add mushrooms, salt, and pepper. Cover and sauté over low heat until mushrooms are tender.
3. In a separate pan combine tamari and molasses or brown sauce. Blend well and add soybeans. Cover and cook over low heat for approximately 10 minutes.
4. Combine soybean mixture with mushrooms and stir well. Top with dill and serve immediately.

MENU SUGGESTION
Serve with buttered noodles or macaroni.

MARINATED TEMPEH

servings: 4
preparation time: 1 hour (not including
  defrosting)

    4 garlic cloves, pressed
    4 scallions, chopped fine
    1 tablespoon grated ginger
      juice of one lemon
    1 teaspoon honey or molasses
    2 tb. vegetable or olive oil
    ¼ cup tamari soy sauce
    ¼ teaspoon nutmeg
      cayenne pepper (to taste)
    1 pound tempeh, defrosted

1. Combine all ingredients, except tempeh, and mix well.
2. Cut tempeh in chunks or slice into steak-like pieces.
3. Marinate tempeh in sauce for an hour or longer. Then grill, barbecue or broil, basting with marinade until browned (about 5 minutes on each side.)

VARIATION
This sauce can be used with firm tofu in the same way or stir-fried; also on grilled or stir-fried vegetables.

CHAPTER

6

I think you will be surprised at all the types of
sandwiches and appetizers that may be made
replace (or augment) the old standbys.

Vegetable or bean spreads make good sandwich fillings; a large quantity can be prepared
at one time and stored in the refrigerator. Make

Sandwiches, Appetizers, and Hors d' Oeuvres

free use of the many nut butters available, such
as peanut, cashew, sesame and almond. They are
delicious alone or in combination with other
ingredients.

Again—invent, experiment and enjoy the
results!

EGG AND AVOCADO SPREAD

servings: 4
preparation time: 10 minutes (not including chilling)

  1 large ripe avocado
  4 hard-cooked eggs
  1 tablespoon mayonnaise (approxi-
    mately)
  ½ large or 1 small onion, chopped fine
  ½ large or 1 small apple, chopped fine
    pinch each of mustard powder and
      garlic salt
    salt and pepper to taste

  1. Mash avocado and eggs well.
  2. Add remaining ingredients and mix
     well. Chill and use as a sandwich
     spread.

NOTE
Stored in a tight container, this spread
keeps well in the refrigerator for future
use.

VARIATION
To use as a dip, increase the amount of
mayonnaise.

HUMUS (CHICK-PEA SPREAD)

servings: 4
preparation time: 5 minutes

    1 cup chick peas, cooked
    1 cup tahini (sesame butter)
    2 tablespoons olive oil
       juice of 2 lemons
    2 garlic cloves, pressed
       salt to taste
       chopped parsley

1. Mash chick peas well in a blender or food processor.
2. Combine with remaining ingredients, except parsley, and mix well. Spread on bread or crackers, or serve as an appetizer on lettuce. Garnish with parsley.

NOTE
To use as a dip, increase the amount of olive oil, or add water.

EGGPLANT SPREAD

servings: 4
preparation time: 40 minutes (not including chilling)

     1 large eggplant
     1 onion, chopped
     1 green pepper, chopped
  1½ tablespoons olive oil
     1 large apple, peeled and cored
     2 hard-cooked eggs (optional)
     1 tablespoon lemon juice
    12 black olives, pitted and chopped fine
       salt to taste
       pinch of chili powder

1. Bake eggplant in 350° oven until
   very soft.
2. Meanwhile, sauté onion and green
   pepper lightly in ½ tablespoon oil.
   Allow to cool.
3. Grate apple and eggs together.
4. Remove skin and seeds from eggplant; drain well and mash until
   fluffy.
5. Combine all ingredients. Mix well and
   chill. Use as a sandwich spread, or
   serve as an appetizer on lettuce.

NOTE
Omit eggs if spread is to be refrigerated
for a lengthy period.

GUACAMOLE

servings: 2
preparation time: 5 minutes (not including chilling)

      salt to taste
   1 garlic clove, cut in half
   1 large ripe avocado
   ½ onion, chopped fine
   ½ teaspoon chili powder
   ¼ teaspoon mustard powder
   1 teaspoon lemon juice
      mayonnaise

1. Sprinkle salt in a bowl and rub in
   garlic.
2. Mash avocado well and combine with
   remaining ingredients, except
   mayonnaise.
3. Spread a layer of mayonnaise on top
   and chill. Blend in mayonnaise just
   before serving. Use as a sandwich
   spread or serve as an appetizer on
   lettuce.

TOFUMOLE

This is a high-protein dip or spread

servings: 4
preparation time: 5 minutes

    1 large ripe avocado
    8 oz. soft tofu
    ½ onion chopped fine
    1 tomato, chopped fine
    2 garlic cloves, pressed
      juice of one lemon
    1 teaspoon (or more to taste) chili
        powder
      salt to taste (optional)

1. Mash avocado and tofu together until smooth.
2. Combine mixture with remaining ingredients and mix well (you may use
   a blender or food processor).
3. Serve with chips, crackers, or raw
   vegetables (crudités.)

VEGETARIAN CHOPPED "LIVER"

serving: 1½ pounds
preparation time: 30 minutes (not including chilling)

2 large onions, chopped
4 garlic cloves, minced
8 ounces mushrooms, sliced
1 tablespoon sesame oil
1 pound (4 cups) walnuts
2 hard boiled eggs
  tamari soy sauce and pepper (to
    taste)
1 tablespoon fenugreek powder
  chopped parsley or dill as garnish

1. Sauté onions, garlic and mushrooms in oil until onions are golden.
2. Combine with remaining ingredients (except garnish) and blend in food processor until consistency of chopped liver. Adjust seasonings if necessary. Sprinkle garnish on top.
3. Serve chilled with crackers, thin slices of bread; or on bed of lettuce leaves.

NOTE
This is extremely rich; a little goes a long way. It is great for a buffet party.

SHOSHANA'S MOCK LIVER PATE

yield: 4 cups
preparation time: 1 hour

    3 medium carrots, sliced
    8 green beans, sliced
    1 medium onion, sliced
    3 stalks celery, sliced
    ½ cup mushrooms, sliced
    2 cups firm tofu (3 cakes)
    ½ tablespoon each fresh basil, parsley
        and thyme
    3 tablespoons lemon juice or cider
        vinegar
        cayenne pepper to taste (optional)
        salt and pepper to taste
    2 tablespoons oil

1. Steam vegetables until soft. Reserve water.
2. Blend vegetables with remaining ingredients until very smooth. Mixture should be thick but able to spread on crackers or bread. If not thick enough, add a small amount of rice flour or finely ground bread crumbs. If too thick, add water from vegetables.

NOTE
The best consistency is achieved by refrigerating for at least 20 minutes before serving.

MUSHROOM AND CELERY APPETIZER

servings: 4
preparation time: 5 minutes (not including chilling)

½ pound whole small mushrooms or
    large mushroom caps
4 stalks celery, cut in large chunks
1 small jar capers, drained
2 tablespoons olive oil
1 tablespoon cider vinegar
    pinch of thyme

1. Blanch mushrooms and celery by stirring in boiling water for approximately 2 minutes (blanching keeps mushrooms white). Remove quickly from water.
2. Combine with all remaining ingredients and mix well. Chill and serve with crackers or flat bread.

VARIATION
This dish can become a mealtime salad by increasing the amounts of mushrooms and celery.

VEGETABLE PÂTÉ

yield: canapés for 10, or 4 sandwiches
preparation time: 30 minutes (not including chilling)

   2 tablespoons butter or oil
   2 yellow onions, chopped
   4 small white onions (or 1 large Ber-
      muda onion), chopped
   ½ pound shallots, sliced
   2 garlic cloves, minced
   1 pound mushrooms, sliced
      pinch each of coriander, cardamom,
      and pepper
   ½ teaspoon curry powder
      salt to taste
      bunch of fresh dill, chopped

1. Using half the butter or oil, sauté
   onions, shallots, and garlic over medium heat until pale yellow.
2. Add mushrooms, seasoning (except
   dill), and remaining butter. Lower
   heat, cover, and sauté until
   mushrooms are tender.
3. Remove from heat and allow to cool
   slightly; then place in blender and
   purée.
4. Transfer to a bowl or dish, top with
   dill, and chill until ready to serve.
5. Serve with crackers or flat bread; or,
   with lettuce, as a sandwich spread.

NOTE
Pâté will keep well for several days when
stored in a tight container and
refrigerated.

CREAM CHEESE AND APPLE SANDWICH

Between two slices of whole-wheat or corn bread, place a layer each of cream cheese, wafer-thin apple slices, and chopped walnuts or almonds. Top with a few sprigs of watercress or fresh mint.

CHEDDAR-AVOCADO-SPROUTS SANDWICH

Spread nut butter on a slice of whole-wheat bread. Place on top: 2 thin slices each of avocado and tomato and a thick slice of sharp Cheddar cheese. Melt butter in a pan and grill, covered, over low heat until cheese melts. Sprinkle liberally with alfalfa sprouts and serve hot with a fork and knife.

COLD ASPARAGUS SANDWICH

Between two slices of whole-wheat or homemade white bread, place cold cooked asparagus, Russian dressing, a few slices of pimiento, and a sprinkling of toasted sesame seeds.

C H A P T E R

7

Use stone-ground whole-grain flours whenever possible. Try to avoid enriched white flour and replace it with whole-wheat, corn, rye, soy, oatmeal, wheat germ or combinations of them. Whole-wheat pastry flour can be obtained for baking requiring finer flour.

Here are some hints for adapting white flour recipes to whole-wheat:

1. Sift flour at least 3 times.

Breads, Cakes, and Cookies

2. One cup of white flour equals ¾ cup of whole-wheat flour.
3. Whole-wheat flour requires more liquid (approximately ¼ more) and slightly less oil, depending upon the texture.
4. Replace white sugar with honey or molasses (use ⅔ quantity called for). Whole-wheat flours vary, so adjust amounts according to the type being used.

CHAPATTIS (INDIAN FLAT BREAD)

yield: 8 large chapattis
preparation time: 15 minutes.

2 cups whole-wheat flour
1 teaspoon salt
2 tablespoons toasted sesame seeds
water

1. Mix dry ingredients together.
2. Pour in enough water to make dough pliable and knead well. Add just enough water for dough to have skinlike texture and continue kneading, roughly, until dough is a smooth and elastic ball.
3. Pinch off a small piece of dough, form into a small ball, and roll continuously on a floured board into a very thin circle of dough. Repeat until all dough is used.
4. Heat a griddle or frying pan very hot. Put chapatti on for approximately ½ minute on each side. (Dough "blisters" slightly and brown marks appear.)
5. Flip onto warmed plate, cover with cloth to keep warm, and repeat process until all chapattis are cooked.
6. Butter lightly and serve.

CRACKERS

yield: depends on size
preparation time: 20 minutes

 1 cup whole wheat flour
¼ cup cornmeal, wheatmeal, or Scottish oatmeal (or whole wheat flour)
 1 teaspoon low-sodium baking powder (optional)
 1 teaspoon salt
⅓ cup oil
¼ cup milk

1. Sift all of the dry ingredients together.
2. Cut in the oil thoroughly.
3. Add the milk in the same fashion as for pastry crust, quickly and without much handling.
4. Form into several balls and roll out to ⅛ inch thickness. Cut out with biscuit or cookie cutters into a variety of shapes.
5. Bake on slightly greased baking sheet in 375 degree oven for 8–10 minutes. Don't overbake.

VARIATIONS
Add any of the following seeds: sesame, caraway, poppy, or dill; or very finely chopped onions or grated cheese. Sprinkle these over the top of the dough and press them in gently before cutting the crackers out.

MATZO MEAL DUMPLINGS

yield: about 30 dumplings
preparation time: 30 minutes

      5 potatoes, cooked, peeled, and
         mashed
      5 eggs
      5 teaspoons salt
   1¼ cup oil
   1¼ cup matzo meal

1. Mix all ingredients together
   thoroughly.
2. Form into balls the size of a small
   egg.
3. Drop balls into boiling salted water.
   Cook until dumplings expand and
   float to the surface, approximately
   20 minutes.
4. Serve in any clear or puréed vegetable soup.

NOTE
Dumpling mixture can be kept in
refrigerator, covered, until ready to cook.

MATZO MEAL ROLLS

yield: 12 rolls
preparation time: 1 hour

1½ cups water
½ cup vegetable or seed oil
1 teaspoon honey
½ teaspoon salt
2 cups matzo meal
4 eggs

1. Preheat oven to 450°.
2. Combine water, oil, honey, and salt, and bring to a boil.
3. Remove from heat and immediately add matzo meal, beating well.
4. Allow mixture to cool; then add eggs, one at a time, beating continuously.
5. Grease a cookie sheet well. Drop on mixture by tablespoonfuls.
6. Bake at 450° for 10 minutes, then lower oven to 350° and bake for an additional 25 minutes. These rolls taste best when served warm.

RYE BREAD

yield: 2 loaves
preparation time: 3½ hours

2 envelopes (1 ounce) dry yeast
½ cup warm water
1 tablespoon salt
3 tablespoons caraway seeds
½ cup molasses (light)
1 cup warm water
2 tablespoons vegetable or seed oil
2 cups all-purpose flour, sifted
3 cups rye flour, sifted
oil

1. Mix yeast in ½ cup warm water to soften.
2. Combine salt, caraway seeds, molasses, remaining water, and 2 tablespoons oil; and add yeast.
3. Mix flours and slowly stir into yeast mixture. Knead dough on floured board until very smooth. Form into a ball and place in a greased bowl.

Brush with oil, cover, and place bowl in a warm place. Allow to stand until doubled in size, approximately 1½ hours.
4. Punch down dough and form into a ball again. Cover and allow to stand for 10 minutes.
5. Form into two loaves. Place loaves in greased bread pans. Cover again and allow to rise until doubled in size, approximately 1 hour.
6. Preheat oven to 450°.
7. Brush loaves lightly with water or egg yolk and bake for 10 min. Lower heat to 350° and bake ½ hour longer.
8. Allow crust to become brown, and then cover with foil or paper to prevent burning.

BASIC WHOLE-WHEAT BREAD

yield: 2 loaves
preparation time: 2 hours

7 cups whole-wheat flour
1 tablespoon salt
½ cup warm water
1 tablespoon honey or molasses
2 envelopes (1 ounce) dry yeast
2 cups warm water

1. Mix flour and salt in a large bowl.
2. Heat oven to about 200° and put bowl in, leaving oven door open, for approximately 10 minutes.
3. Meanwhile, mix yeast, ½ cup warm water, and honey in a bowl; keep warm on top of stove for 15 minutes.
4. Grease 2 cookie sheets or baking pans.
5. Take flour from oven and stir in yeast mixture (which should be bubbly). Gradually stir in 2 cups of warm water, and knead 5–10 minutes.
6. Shape into two loaves and place on cookie sheets or in bread pans.
7. Place on top shelf of warm oven, half-closing door, and allow to rise for approximately 20 minutes.
8. Increase heat to 375°, close door, and bake for 45 minutes.
9. At the end of baking time, tap bottoms of loaves. If they sound hollow, they are done. Bake a few minutes more if not done.
10. Cool loaves on rack.

VARIATION
1 cup raisins may be added before baking.

UNYEASTED WHOLE-WHEAT BREAD WITH FRUIT AND NUTS

yield: 1 large or 2 small loaves
preparation time: 1½ hours

3 cups whole-wheat flour
1 cup corn flour
½ cup chopped hazelnuts
½ cup chopped raisins
1 teaspoon salt
2 teaspoons cinnamon
1 egg yolk
1 cup water (approximately)

1. Preheat oven to 350°.
2. Mix all ingredients (except water) together with hands.
3. Add water slowly and knead well until dough is smooth and has skinlike texture. Add more water if necessary.
4. Shape into loaf or loaves, brush a bit of egg yolk or water on top, and place in a greased pan or on a cookie sheet. Bake for approximately 1 hour.

VARIATIONS

CARROTS: Use same ingredients and procedure as above, but omit fruit, nuts, and cinnamon and substitute two carrots cut into "matchsticks" (see page 74) and sautéed in 1 teaspoon oil.

ONIONS: Use same ingredients and procedure as in first variation, but omit carrots and substitute two onions, sliced and sautéed in 1 teaspoon oil.

CARROT TORTE

yield: 1 10-inch torte
preparation time: 1 hour

 12 eggs, separated
 ½ cup honey or ¾ cup date sugar
 6 tablespoons grated carrot
 6 tablespoons grated apple
 6 tablespoons grated almonds
 3 tablespoons flour
 1 teaspoon lemon juice
   pinch of salt

1. Preheat oven to 375°.
2. Mix egg yolks and sweetener together until pale yellow. Add apple, carrot, and almonds. Fold in flour. Add lemon juice.
3. Whip egg whites and salt stiff, and fold into batter.
4. Grease a 10-inch cake pan (spring form, if possible) and sprinkle with a little flour or wheat germ. Pour in batter and bake until an inserted knife comes out dry, approximately 45 minutes.

FRUIT AND NUT CAKE

yield: 1 9-inch cake
preparation time: 1 hour

  1 ¾ cup flour
  1 teaspoon baking soda
  ½ teaspoon salt
  1 teaspoon cinnamon
  ½ teaspoon nutmeg
  ½ cup honey
  ¼ cup oil
  1 egg, beaten
  1 cup toasted and chopped almonds
  1 cup chopped raisins
  1 cup applesauce, warm

1. Preheat oven to 350°.
2. Sift flour, soda, salt, cinnamon, and nutmeg together.
3. In a separate bowl, blend honey and oil well, then beat in egg.
4. Stir dry ingredients into honey and oil mixture gradually, and beat until smooth.
5. Add nuts, raisins, and applesauce; beat well.
6. Pour batter into greased 9-inch tube pan and bake for approximately 40 minutes, or until knife inserted in center comes out clean.

VARIATIONS
Try experimenting with other fruits and nuts such as apricots, oranges, dates, and walnuts.

JELLY ROLL

yield: 1 roll
preparation time: 30 minutes

  4 eggs, separated
½ teaspoon salt
  1 cup date sugar
  1 teaspoon baking powder
  1 cup flour
  1 teaspoon almond or vanilla extract
    jam or jelly

1. Preheat oven to 375°.
2. Whip egg whites with half of salt until almost stiff, then fold in sugar.
3. Beat egg yolks with remaining salt
   until pale yellow and add to egg
   whites mixture.
4. Sift other dry ingredients together
   into mixture, add flavoring, and mix
   well.
5. Line a jelly roll pan with aluminum
   foil. Pour in mixture evenly and bake
   for approximately 15 minutes.
6. Remove from oven and carefully
   strip off foil. Place cake right side up
   on waxed paper, spread with jam or
   jelly, and roll into a log.
7. Place waxed paper around log until
   set.

VARIATION
Ice cream may also be used as filling: Roll
cake in wax paper and, when cool, unroll
and fill with ice cream. Place in freezer
until ready to serve.

PEANUT BUTTER COOKIES

yield: depends on size
preparation time: 1½ hours

¼ pound butter
1 cup peanut butter
1 cup honey
1 teaspoon vanilla
1 pound whole wheat flour
1 teaspoon salt

1. Cream butters, honey and vanilla.
2. Combine the flour and salt, and blend these two mixtures.
3. Refrigerate the dough for 1 hour, slice, and bake for 15–20 minutes at 450 degrees. (Press a fork into the cookies before baking.)

SUNFLOWER MEAL COOKIES

yield: about 14 cookies
preparation time: 40 minutes

¾ cup sunflower meal
¼ cup wheat germ
2 tablespoons honey
2 tablespoons oil
1 egg, beaten well
½ tart apple, grated
    pinch of salt

1. Preheat oven to 350°.
2. Mix all ingredients together well with beater or wooden spoon.
3. Grease a cookie sheet and drop batter by tablespoonfuls.
4. Bake for ½ hour. Remove from sheet and allow to cool before serving.

CHAPTER

8

Sauces and dressings can transform simple vegetables and salads into gourmet masterpieces. There are many sauces and dressings that can be adapted to vegetarian cookery. The few I have chosen for inclusion here are generally made from natural ingredients and are quick and easy to prepare.

Sauces and dressings are greatly enhanced by the addition of seeds, nuts and herbs. Check with

Sauces and Dressings

A Glossary of Herbs (pages 17–19) to find out which herb goes best with which fruit or vegetable. Egg yolks are a delicious, rich thickener for sauces.

Try to be discriminating when using sauces. If your dishes are made from good-quality wholesome ingredients, the sauces should be used as a complement and not as a disguise.

BASIC CREAM SAUCE

yield: ¾ cup
preparation time: 10 minutes

  2 tablespoons butter or oil
  2 tablespoons flour
½ cup milk or ¾ cup light sweet
     cream, at room temperature
   salt and pepper to taste
   pinch of nutmeg

1. Melt butter or heat oil in a double
   boiler or small pan over low heat.
2. Add flour and stir constantly with a
   wooden spoon.
3. Gradually pour in milk or cream, stirring constantly, until mixture thickens. Sauce should be smooth—if
   lumpy, beat well with a beater. Season and serve hot.

NOTE
If a thinner sauce is desired, add more
milk or cream and stir well.

VARIATIONS
For a cheese sauce: Add ½ cup grated
Cheddar or combination Cheddar and
American cheese to sauce after adding
milk. Cheese shoould be thoroughly melted and sauce smooth.
    To make this dairy-free, substitute ¾
cup of soymilk for milk or cream and
blend in ¼ cup soft tofu. Heat through.

BROWN SAUCE

yield: 1½ cups
preparation time: 10 minutes

    2 tablespoons butter or vegetable oil
    1 small onion, chopped (optional)
    2 tablespoons flour or arrowroot
    1 cup boiling water
    1 tablespoon or 1 envelope instant
        vegetable broth (preferably dark)
      salt and pepper to taste
      pinch each of thyme and ginger
    1 tablespoon tamari sauce

1. In a small pan, melt butter and sauté onion (if used) lightly.
2. Over low heat, add flour and stir constantly with a wooden spoon until lightly browned.
3. Dissolve broth in boiling water and gradually pour into flour mixture. Continue stirring until mixture thickens. Sauce should be smooth; if lumpy, beat well with a beater.
4. Stir in seasoning and tamari sauce. Serve hot over vegetables, rice, grain, or pasta.

NOTE
Puréed vegetable soup or cooked vegetable stock can be substituted for instant vegetable broth.

SPECIAL BROWN SAUCE

yield: 1 quart
preparation time: ½ hour

  ½ pound mushrooms
  1 large onion, chopped
  2 tablespoons butter or oil
  2 cups water or vegetable broth
  2 tablespoons grain coffee substitute
  ½ cup arrowroot
  2 tablespoons tamari sauce
  4 tomatoes, chopped (optional)

1. Sauté mushrooms and onion in butter or oil.
2. Add 1 cup water or broth, bring to boil and simmer gently for about 15 minutes.
3. Add grain "coffee" and blend well.
4. Dilute arrowroot in remaining water or broth and add slowly, stirring continuously.
5. Add tamari and stir; then add tomatoes. Serve hot over grains, vegetables, nut loaves, beans, etc.

MISO AND TAHINI SAUCE

yield: ¼–½ cup
preparation time: 10 minutes

1 tablespoon miso (soybean paste)
2 tablespoons tahini (sesame butter)
1 teaspoon grated orange peel
1 tablespoon arrowroot or flour
    water

1. Blend miso and tahini together and add orange peel.
2. Over low heat, combine with arrowroot or flour; stir well until thickened.
3. Add water (amount of water will depend on consistency desired), blend well, and simmer. Serve hot or cold with vegetables or citrus fruits.

VARIATION
This sauce can be converted into a delicious sandwich spread in the following manner: Increase tahini to 4 tablespoons. Omit arrowroot or flour, and add only 1 or 2 tablespoons water. Cook 5 minutes until thickened. Cool and serve.

TAMARI AND TAHINI SAUCE

yield: ¼ cup
preparation time: 10 minutes

    1 onion, chopped
    1 teaspoon oil
    1 tablespoon tamari sauce
    1 tablespoon tahini (sesame butter)
    arrowroot or flour (to thicken)
    water

1. Sauté onion in oil until tender.
2. Blend tamari and tahini together and proceed as for Miso and Tahini Sauce (see page 149).
3. Serve hot with cooked vegetables.

SWEET AND SOUR SAUCE FOR VEGETABLES

yield: 1 quart
preparation time: ½ hour

  1 tablespoon oil
½ cup acid fruit juice (pineapple,
    grapefruit or orange)
  1 cup vegetable broth or water
½ teaspoon salt
  2 tablespoons arrowroot
  2 tablespoons vinegar
  1 teaspoon grated ginger
  2 tablespoons honey or rice syrup

1. Bring oil, juice, water or broth and salt to a boil.
2. Thicken with arrowroot and remove from heat.
3. Add vinegar, ginger, and honey, stirring well.
4. Cover and keep warm over low heat without reboiling, for about 15 minutes.
5. Keep covered until serving, otherwise some of the piquancy will be lost. This sauce goes well with beets and cooked beans, as well as other vegetables.

VARIATION
Add finely chopped onions and peppers.

MUSTARD-HONEY SALAD DRESSING

yield: ½ cup
preparation time: 5 minutes

 4 tablespoons olive oil
 3 tablespoons lemon juice or vinegar
 1 tablespoon honey
 1 teaspoon mustard powder diluted
    with 1 teaspoon cold water
 1 garlic clove, pressed
   salt and pepper to taste

Combine all ingredients and blend well.

GREEN SAUCE

yield: 1½ cups
preparation time: 5 minutes

½ cup olive or seed oil
¼ cup vinegar
   pinch of mustard powder
2 hard-cooked eggs, whites chopped,
   yolks mashed
3 shallots, chopped fine
2 tablespoons coarsely chopped capers
¼ cup chopped mixed fresh green
   herbs: basil, mint, tarragon, thyme,
   dill
¼ cup chopped parsley

Blend or shake all ingredients well and
chill.
Serve over cooked asparagus or as a
salad dressing.

TOMATO SAUCE

yield: 4 cups
preparation time: 2½ hours

2 large onions, diced
2 stalks celery, diced
1 green pepper, diced
1 garlic clove, minced
2 tablespoons olive oil
4 large ripe tomatoes, cut in large
   chunks, or 1 large can tomatoes
1 can tomato paste
1 cup water (approximately)
1 teaspoon oregano
¼ teaspoon sweet basil
2 teaspoons honey or rice syrup
   salt and pepper to taste
¼ cup grated Parmesan cheese (optional)

1. In a large frying pan, sauté onions, celery, pepper, and garlic in olive oil until lightly browned.
2. Add remaining ingredients and, stirring constantly, bring to a light boil. Cover and let simmer for approximately 2 hours.

VARIATION
For Mushroom-Tomato Sauce, sauté 1 cup sliced mushrooms with other vegetables.

TAHINI DRESSING FOR GREEN SALADS

yield: 1 cup
preparation time: 5 minutes

   ½ cup olive oil
   4 tablespoons tahini (sesame butter)
   2 tablespoons lemon juice
   2 garlic cloves, minced
      salt and pepper to taste

Combine all ingredients in a blender and
blend well.

FRENCH DRESSING

yield: ¾ cup
preparation time: 5 minutes

    ½ cup olive oil
    ¼ cup cider or tarragon vinegar
       juice of ½ lemon
     1 garlic clove, pressed
    ½ teaspoon mustard powder
    ½ teaspoon tamari sauce
       honey to taste
       salt and pepper to taste

Blend or shake all ingredients well and
chill.
Pour over salads or cold vegetables.

NOTE
It might be convenient to make three or
four times the quantity of this recipe
and store it in a large bottle with a tight
cover. It will keep in the refrigerator for a
long time.

MAYONNAISE DRESSING

yield: ¼ cup
preparation time: 5 minutes

    4 tablespoons mayonnaise
      juice of ½ lemon
      pinch each of mustard and curry
        powders
      dash of tamari sauce
      salt and pepper to taste

Blend all ingredients well and chill.
Pour over salads or cold vegetables.

TOFU MAYO

yield: 2 cups
preparation time: 5 minutes (does not include chilling)

½ cup unsaturated fat-free vegetable oil
1 tablespoon vinegar
1 tablespoon lemon juice
1 pound soft tofu
1 egg yolk (optional)
¼ teaspoon honey
½ teaspoon mustard
   salt or salt-free seasoning or tamari soy sauce (to taste)
   teaspoon chopped garlic or onion (optional)

1. Pour oil, vinegar and lemon juice a blender or food processor and blend.
2. Slowly add tofu and egg yolk, blending constantly.
3. Add remaining ingredients and blend until very smooth. Adjust seasonings and chill.

NOTE
This is both low-calorie and cholesterol free (without the egg yolk). This should keep for up to a week in the refrigerator.

VARIATION
To turn this into a salad dressing, add equal amounts of oil and vinegar or lemon and blend well.

ORANGE TAHINI DRESSING

yield: 2 cups
preparation time: 10 minutes

    4 peeled oranges
    2 heaping tablespoons tahini
    1 level tablespoon honey
    1 tablespoon tamari sauce
    1 tablespoon vegetable oil

Blend fruit, tahini, honey, and tamari in blender for 4–5 minutes. Then pour in oil slowly. Blend well.

CHAPTER

9

Fruit is so full of vitamins that it has become a delicious necessity. Fruit, like vegetables, should be organically grown and free of sprays, preservatives and coloring. When in doubt, peel the skins.

The fruit desserts in this chapter include cooked or dried fruit; raw fruit should precede the meal.

Desserts and Beverages

It is necessary to give new thought to beverages; somehow most carbonated drinks, with their artificial colorings, sweeteners, etc., seem out of place with this kind of food. I hope you will use the beverage recipes as suggestions and let your imagination be the only limit to the drinks you can create.

LOUISE'S KANTEN (GELATIN)

servings: 8–10
preparation time: 30 minutes (not including chilling)

1½ cups water or fruit juice
2 bars (6 tablespoons flakes) agar-agar
2⅓ pints fresh strawberries
   maple syrup to taste
1 banana

1. Bring water or juice to boil, add agar-agar and stir until dissolved.
2. Add strawberries and maple syrup and cook over low heat until fruit is cooked.
3. Place mixture immediately in blender with banana and blend until smooth.
4. Place in mold and refrigerate.
5. When thoroughly set and chilled, slice into portions with sharp knife. Decorate with fresh strawberries.

CZECHOSLOVAKIAN CRÊPES
(POLATCHINKY)

yield: 6 large crêpes
preparation time: 30 minutes

1 cup milk
6 tablespoons flour
1 egg, beaten
½ teaspoon baking powder
1 lemon rind, grated
  pinch of salt
  vegetable or seed oil

1. Combine all ingredients (except oil) and mix well.
2. Oil a frying pan very lightly and heat over medium heat.
3. Pour in 1 ladleful of batter and tilt pan until batter covers bottom entirely. Allow a thin layer of batter to adhere to bottom of pan and quickly pour the excess back into bowl. Prick with a knife while cooking, so that pancake will not rise. Cook quickly— approximately 2 minutes for each side—and remove crêpe to a warm plate. Repeat the process until all batter is used.
4. Spread crêpes with jam or nuts and cinnamon and roll or fold sides over into envelope shape. Serve warm.

APRICOT FREEZE

servings: 4
preparation time: 10 minutes (not including freezing)

    1 pound dried apricots, soaked until soft
    1 cup honey
    3 egg whites, stiffly beaten

1. Purêe apricots and honey together in blender.
2. Fold in egg whites.
3. Pour into a greased mold or ice tray(s) and freeze. Serve frozen.

BLUEBERRY TOFU WHIP

servings: 6
preparation time: 10 minutes (not including chilling)

1 pound soft tofu
2 teaspoons vanilla
2 tablespoons lemon juice
1 10-ounce package frozen blueberries
    or 2 cups fresh fruit
1 ripe banana
½ cup honey plus 1 tablespoon maple
    syrup
pinch of salt (optional)

1. Combine tofu, vanilla and lemon juice.
2. Drain juice from blueberries and add to mixture.
3. Place mixture in blender or food processor and blend until creamy.
4. Place in mold or individual dishes and chill well before serving.

VARIATIONS
You can vary the fruit in this recipe by substituting other fresh or frozen berries in the same quantities as above. This recipe can also be made into a nutritious and delicious drink by adding either water, carbonated water, or milk.

MENU SUGGESTION
Serve as dessert or snack, especially with a meal containing a grain dish to create a complementary protein.

CAROB PUDDING

servings: 4
preparation time: ½ hour
    (not including cooling)

2 cups milk
3 tablespoons cornstarch or arrowroot
2 tablespoons carob powder
2 tablespoons honey or maple syrup
    pinch salt
1 teaspoon vanilla

1. Mix ½ cup milk with the cornstarch.
2. Mix another ½ cup milk with the carob, heating it over low heat until it is dissolved into a paste. Stir honey into this mixture.
3. Heat remaining milk to the boiling point and stir in honey-carob mixture. Simmer for 5 minutes.
4. Remove from heat and stir in cornstarch mixture and salt. Return to heat and simmer over an asbestos pad for 5 minutes, stirring until mixture is thick and creamy and carob is well mixed.
5. Remove from heat and add vanilla extract. Cool for several hours.

VARIATIONS
1. Add 2–3 tablespoons mint extract with vanilla extract for carob-mint. Sprinkle top with chopped roasted nuts or sunflower or pumpkin seeds.
2. Mix chopped nuts or seeds into the actual pudding.
3. Top with whipped cream.

FRUIT DUMPLINGS

yield: about 25 dumplings
preparation time: 40 minutes

3 medium potatoes, peeled and cut in
    large chunks
2 eggs, beaten well
2¾ cups flour
    salt to taste
1 pound fresh apricots
1 pound fresh plums
    butter, softened
    bread crumbs
    cinnamon

1. Boil potatoes and mash with a little water and eggs.
2. Combine potato mixture with flour and salt. Beat into a smooth dough.
3. Roll dough until approximately ½ inch thick. Turn a large glass upside down, dip rim in flour, and, using rim, cut dough into circles.
4. Remove stones from fruits and fill each cavity with a scant teaspoon of honey.
5. Place a fruit in center of each circle and fold dough over fruit to make a ball. Roll between hands to smooth out.
6. Drop balls carefully into boiling salted water and cook until dumplings rise to surface, approximately 5 minutes.
7. Mix cinnamon with enough bread crumbs to cover dumplings. Roll dumplings gently first in bread crumbs and then in butter.
8. Place dumplings in a casserole and bake in a warm (350°) oven until browned. Serve hot, with or without a fruit sauce.

NOTE
Dumplings may be prepared in advance and chilled, uncooked.

NUTTY PEACHES

servings: 4
preparation time: 15 minutes

 4 large cooked peach halves
 1 tablespoon butter, melted
 ½ cup chopped nuts
 2 tablespoons honey
 ½ teaspoon cinnamon

1. Brush peach halves with butter.
2. Fill with nuts and sprinkle honey and cinnamon on top.
3. Broil about 3 inches from heat for 10 minutes.
4. Serve hot, with whipped cream if desired.

OLD-FASHIONED STEWED FRUIT

servings: 6–8
preparation time: 1 hour (not including chilling)

2 cups water
2 tablespoons honey or maple syrup (optional)
juice and pulp of 1 lemon
3 pounds fresh pears, peaches, or apricots

1. Boil water with honey or maple syrup and lemon until syrupy, approximately ½ hour
2. Peel fruit, cut in halves, and remove stones.
3. Cook fruit in syrup on medium heat for 15 minutes.
4. Chill and serve plain or with cream.

RHUBARB CRISP

servings: 4–6
preparation time: 1 hour

    4 cups rhubarb, sliced small
    ½ cup orange juice
    ½ cup honey or maple syrup
    1 tablespoon grated orange rind
    1 tablespoon grated lemon rind
    ⅓ cup butter or oil
    2 cups coarse bread crumbs or grain
            cereal (see page 180).

1. Preheat oven to 350°.
2. Place rhubarb in greased baking dish and add orange juice.
3. Combine sugar or honey, orange, and lemon rinds. Sprinkle evenly over rhubarb.
4. Cut butter into bread crumbs or Grain Cereal with two knives until mixture is crumbly. Spread on top of rhubarb.
5. Bake for approximately 45 minutes, until rhubarb is tender. Serve hot or cold.

YOGHURT AND APPLE DRINK

yield: 6 cups
preparation time: 5 minutes

   2 cups yoghurt
   2 cups apple juice
   2 cups water
   ¼ teaspoon cinnamon

Combine all ingredients and blend well.
Serve chilled.

NOTE
Fresh milk can be substituted for water
for a richer beverage.

VARIATION
Substitute 2 cups of any fruit yoghurt
for plain yoghurt, and use 2 cups of a
compatible fruit juice in place of apple
juice. Omit cinnamon, and add honey if
desired.

RICE TEA

yield: 4 cups
preparation time: 25 minutes

½ cup rice
4 cups water

1. Pan-toast rice over high heat, stirring constantly, until browned.
2. Add water, bring to a boil, and simmer for approximately 15 minutes.
3. Strain and serve.

NOTE
This tea can be chilled and served with ice cubes.

VARIATION
Wheat berry can be substituted for rice.

MILK AND FRUIT DRINK

yield: 4 glasses
preparation time: 5 minutes

  ¼ cup powdered milk
  1 quart orange juice
  1 orange, peeled and cut
  1 tablespoon honey

Blend all ingredients with ice in a blender; serve cold, with additional ice if desired.

VARIATIONS
Using a base of ¼ cup powdered milk, blend the following.

BERRIES: Use 1 quart water, 1 cup fresh berries, 1 tablespoon honey, 1 tablespoon lemon juice, and a pinch of mint.

APRICOTS: Use 1 pound dried soaked apricots, 2 cups water (in which apricots were soaked), 2 cups any fruit juice, 1 tablespoon honey, and a dash of vanilla.

LEMON-LIME: Use the juice of ½ lemon and 2 limes, 3 cups water, and 4 tablespoons honey.

BANANA: Use 2 ripe bananas, 4 cups water, 1 teaspoon lemon juice, and 1 tablespoon honey.

BASIC VEGETABLE JUICE COCKTAIL

yield: 5–6 cups
preparation time: 5 minutes

174

1 quart vegetable juice
1 cup water
2 tablespoons lemon juice
2 celery stalks, chopped fine
   salt and pepper to taste

Combine all ingredients and purée well in blender. Serve chilled.

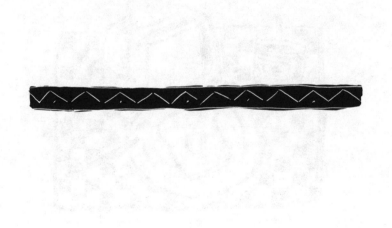

CHAPTER

10

This chapter includes those recipes which don't seem to fit into a specific category; also some sample meals you might want to try.

Potpourri

BASIC NUT LOAF

servings: 6–8
preparation time: 1½ hours

   2 onions, chopped
   ¼ pound mushrooms (optional)
   2 green peppers, chopped
   2 celery stalks, chopped
   1 tablespoon oil
   ½ cup bread crumbs
   ½ cup wheat germ
   2 cups ground nuts
   1 tablespoon brewer's yeast (optional)
   1 tablespoon sage
     Salt and pepper to taste
   2 eggs, beaten
   1 cup milk or soymilk

1. Sauté vegetables lightly in oil.
2. Combine with other ingredients and fill greased baking pans. Bake at 325 degrees for 45 minutes to 1 hour.

VARIATIONS
  1. Replace bread crumbs with cooked grains; adjust liquid for moist consistency.
  2. Powdered milk or half light cream can be substituted for whole milk.
  3. Tomatoes can be substituted for mushrooms and peppers. There is no need to sauté them. Add more bread crumbs or grain if too moist.

NUTS, SEEDS, AND FRUITS

yield: your choice
preparation time: 3 minutes

> sunflower seeds
> roasted salted soybeans
> almonds
> cashews
> raisins or currants
> other dried fruit

Mix together and use as a delicious (and healthy) nibble.

HERB BUTTER

yield: ¼ cup
preparation time: 5 minutes

> 2 tablespoons butter
> 1 tablespoon oil
> 2 garlic cloves, pressed
> 1 tablespoon chopped oregano
> 1 tablespoon chopped basil
> 2 tablespoons grated Parmesan cheese
>   (optional)

Blend all ingredients into a paste and chill for use on vegetables, pasta, bread, etc.
NOTE
Try to use fresh herbs. If those specified above are not available, others may be substituted.

HOMEMADE GRAIN CEREAL

yield: 1½ pounds
preparation time: 30 minutes

3 tablespoons butter or oil
¾ cup honey
1 pound rolled oats
¾ cup sunflower seeds
½–¾ cup whole cashews, almonds, and/or
    hazelnuts
1 cup wheat germ
¼ pound coconut, toasted (optional)
½ cup toasted sesame seeds
½ cup raisins
¼ cup other dried fruit, chopped

1. In a large pan, heat butter or oil and honey over medium heat. Add oats and stir until well-coated with butter or oil.
2. When oats become golden, add sunflower seeds and nuts. Stir well and continue cooking.
3. When mixture begins to brown, add wheat germ and continue cooking for approximately 5 more minutes.
4. Add coconut (if used) and sesame seeds, stirring continuously for another 5 minutes. Mixture should be a rich brown.
5. Turn off heat, leave pan on stove, add fruit, and continue stirring for a few minutes.
6. Remove pan from stove and allow to cool. Store in a plastic bag or jar. Serve for breakfast, snacks, or as a dessert with yoghurt, milk, cream, honey, fresh fruit, or ice cream, etc.

NOTE
This is an excellent substitute for bread crumbs and may be used as a sweet topping or whenever breading is needed.

SHEPHERD'S BREAD*

yield: 6 slices
preparation time: 10 minutes

> 6 slices hard bread or rolls
>   water or milk
> 3 garlic cloves, cut in half
>   oil

Soak bread or rolls in water or milk to soften. Fry garlic in oil until brown; add bread and deep fry on both sides until crispy.

*So-called because it is a favorite dish among shepherds and peasants in southern Europe.

SIMPLE FRUIT JAM

yield: 2 pounds
preparation time: 5 minutes (not including soaking)

    1 pound dried apricots, soaked until
        soft
 1¼ pound honey
    juice and rind of 1 lemon

Squeeze excess water from apricots and
purée all ingredients in a blender. Serve
at once or refrigerate in a tight jar or
jars.

182

VARIATION
Other dried fruits or fresh strawberries
may be substituted for apricots—simply
adjust honey accordingly.

MAKE-YOUR-OWN YOGHURT

yield: 1 quart yoghurt
preparation time: 4 hours

  1 quart milk
  3 tablespoons powdered milk
  1 package yoghurt culture or 3
      tablespoons yoghurt.

1. Combine milk and powdered milk in a pan and bring to a boil. Remove from heat, cover, and cool to luke-warm (about 115°).
2. Add yoghurt culture or yoghurt and stir very well. Pour into prewarmed clean jars. Cap jars and cover with towels to keep warm. Mixture must stay warm; place jars in warm water if necessary.
3. When mixture has thickened to desired consistency, refrigerate jars. Yoghurt is ready to use.

NOTE
For best results, use a high-quality milk and culture (such as Bulgarian) or yoghurt. Make succeeding batches—for up to a month—by adding 3 tablespoons of this yoghurt to milk mixture and repeating process.

SESAME SALT

yield: ¼ cup
preparation time: 20 minutes

    8 tablespoons sesame seeds
    1 tablespoon salt

1. Heat a large frying pan very hot.
2. Toast sesame seeds, stirring continuously with a wooden spoon, until lightly browned.
3. Place seeds and salt in a mortar and crush with a pestle until seeds are finely ground.
4. Return mixture to frying pan and stir over high heat until well browned.
5. Return to mortar and continue crushing mixture with pestle until it becomes a powder.
6. Store in a tight jar and use as a seasoning instead of salt; or as a topping for salad, soup, vegetables, etc.

NOTE
The proportion of eight parts seeds to one part salt is standard; for a saltier taste, it may be increased to six-to-one. Sesame salt should be prepared weekly, as it goes stale after that time. It must be kept dry.

SAMPLE MENUS

Here are some menus derived from recipes in this book:

1. Mixed Fruit Salad (see page 30).
   Artichoke and Egg in Mayonnaise
     (see page 28).
   Couscous with Vegetables (see page
     101).
   Peanut Butter Cookies (see page
     142).
2. Sweet Cream of Carrot Soup (see
     page 42).
   Eggs à la Russe (see page 56).
   Cuban Rice (see page 107).
   French Beans with Sunflower Seeds
     (see page 77).
   Fruit Dumplings (see page 167).
3. Cucumber and Yoghurt Salad (see
     page 29).
   All-Green-Vegetable Soup (see page
     49).
   Middle Eastern Lima Beans (see page
     114).
   Rice in Brown Sauce with
     Mushrooms (see page 148).
   Chapattis (see page 132).
   Apricot Freeze (see page 164).
4. Quick Cold Gazpacho (see page 45).
   Mushroom and Celery Appetizer (see
     page 127).
   Miguel's Authentic Spanish Omelette
     (see page 58).
   Fried Green Peppers (see page 84).
   Fruit and Nut Cake (see page 140).

C H A P T E R

11

Some hostesses (and hosts) think that vegetarian parties present the greatest challenge.

Party Menus

Here are some ideas to make planning easier and fun.

SUMMER BUFFET

Cold Fresh Cherry Soup   (see page 43)
Grapefruit and Avocado Salad
    (see page 31)
Cold Tahini Broccoli   (see page 70)
Vegetarian Chopped Liver
    (see page 125)
Tofumole with blue corn chips
    (see page 124)
Humus with whole wheat pita wedges
    (see page 120)
Louise's Kanten   (see page 162)

188

WINTER FEAST

Vegetable Soup With Wheat Berry
    (see page 50)
Marinated Tempeh   (see page 117)
Persian Rice   (see page 108)
Baked Squash   (see page 90)
Exotic Green Walnut Salad   (see page 35)
Jelly Roll   (see page 141)

INDIAN DINNER

Spicy Indian Dahl Soup   (see page 44)
Indian Pakora   (see page 83)
Chappatis   (see page 132)
Cucumber and Yoghurt Salad
                                (see page 29)
Apricot Freeze   (see page 164)

HEARTY BRUNCH

Gazpacho   (see page 45)
Miguel's Authentic Spanish Omelette
                                (see page 58)
Baked Cheese Pancakes   (see page 61)
Mixed Fruit Salad   (see page 30)

Index

192